GAME
and
BIRD CALLING

A. C. Becker, Jr.

A. S. Barnes and Company

Contents

Introduction

In spite of his super accurate, long-range weapons, man today finds it increasingly difficult to bag his game. A hundred years ago many Americans could bag game within the shadows of the homestead. Fifty years ago the outdoorsman found game a little more removed, but he was still able to hunt reasonably well just beyond the city limits.

Today the American outdoorsman has to cross miles and miles of geometric designs of asphalt, concrete, and steel to reach country suitable for wildlife. But then if the wind is wrong and there hangs over this country a pall of manmade pollution, the outdoorsman will have to penetrate many more miles into the wilderness to find the game he seeks.

All of this travel requires time and money. As an example in my home state of Texas, the deer hunter of 50 years ago could get a hunting lease for ten dollars a season. Today ten dollars will get you hunting privileges for half a day on the big day hunting ranches. Four decades ago the waterfowl hunter could hunt for free. Waterfowl hunting privileges on these same lands today command daily fees ranging from five to 25 dollars.

Not only is the modern hunter faced with a problem of time and money, he has still another handicap, that of less game. The eruption of civilization has greatly diminished wilderness acreage. Consequently there is less game available. Furthermore, most wild game species have learned by association that man is a danger and a threat to their lives. The result has been for surviving wildlife to move ever deeper into the remotest parts of their shrinking wilderness.

If the sportsman expects to be reasonably successful on his hunts, he must get all the help he can find. The most accurate rifle and most powerful ammunition is not going to get the hunter game if the species sought does not reveal its presence. Many animal and bird species respond to sound. When the sounds are right to fit the occasion, many of these game species drop their natural caution and reveal themselves to the hunter.

I have in this book sought to point out why and how wildlife responds to calls and sounds. In addition, two special chapters are included—one concerns how sound can be used to call fish, and the other how to photograph rather than shoot game called.

A. C. Becker, Jr.,
Galveston, Texas

GAME
and
BIRD CALLING

1.

In the Beginning

BECAUSE SELF-PRESERVATION IS THE MOST IMPORTANT AND BASIC of all instincts, it stands to reason that man's oldest activity—not profession—is hunting. He had to hunt to find food in order to sustain life. In the beginning the earliest man was both the hunter and the hunted. For ages hunting was a way of life, and it did not become a sport until recent centuries.

In his quest for game, primitive man's problem was identical with the one that plagues modern man today: getting the game within effective range of the weapon in hand. Earliest man's hunting tools were clubs and stones, and effective range was but a matter of a few yards. With the coming of the spear, and later the arrow, effective range was extended. Still by present-day standards this range was ridiculously short. It meant early man had to get pretty darned close to the beast he sought to kill. He had to stalk his game. He probably augmented his stalking by making guttural sounds, imitating as best he could the sounds made by the creatures he sought. His number one problem was that of getting the animal close enough to slay. He lived in the wild with wildlife, and this in itself gave him an advantage. He intimately knew wilderness inhabitants, their characteristics, and the sounds they made. He knew what smaller creatures they fed upon and he knew the sounds these creatures made. Game was plentiful, but the range of his weapons was woefully short. Nevertheless, he knew how to call to bring his target near.

Modern man has at his disposal a veritable arsenal of weapons, many with extremely long range. Yet he still faces the caveman's problem of getting his game in range. Why? For one thing game is scarcer today. More important is the fact that most game has had enough contact with man to recognize him as a mortal danger. Consequently they give him a wide berth. Modern man, like his early counterpart, is still a hunter, but except for rare cases he is no longer the hunted. Man of many, many centuries ago was not feared by wild beasts for he was hunted by the very creatures he sought. Except for a few remote wilderness areas that still exist in the world where a few wild animals may hunt man, wildlife creatures have come to fear man. As a result, and especially on the North American continent, game steers clear of man.

Today man has long-range weapons, yet he is still faced with the age-old problem of getting his target within effective range. Like his prehistoric predecessor he has learned that certain sounds will arouse various moods to cause game to come closer to him. So he employs game calls to fit his purpose today.

Modern man can read and write and reason, and he has a high capacity for learning and intelligence. In spite of this, early man had the advantage. He knew wildlife sounds because he was surrounded by them. The 20th-century man, too, is surrounded by wildlife, but he is separated from intimacy by a concrete, steel, and asphalt jungle. His ears are bombarded by the roar of city streets, the rhythmic pounding of industry, and the blare of television, interrupted frequently by jangling telephones. His ears are untrained for hearing wildlife, and then when he does hear the sounds he is usually unable to recognize the source or the species.

But today's hunter is intelligent. He can read, understand what he reads, and then apply the knowledge gained. The purpose of this book is to help instruct the city dweller—the fellow in the multi-storied steel and concrete apartment building —in the fine art of wildlife calling.

Bird and animal calling is as old as hunting itself. It has become a refined art in which many sophisticated implements and devices are used. The sport only seems new today because of the large number of magazine and newspaper features on game calling. These, of course, are augmented by a great number of game call advertisements that appear in numerous hunting and outdoors publications. In addition, there have been television and movie shorts on the subject.

Since there are no written records to lend supporting evidence, we can only assume that what bird and game calling prehistoric man did, he did with his own voice, using grunts, groans, and coughs to accomplish his mission. If he used any aids, we can only assume they may have been the hollow bones of birds or the horns of animals he killed.

Throughout recorded history there are only vague references to the calling of birds and animals. But through the years artifacts representing the various centuries have been identified as implements to call game. The most common are the horns of rams, cattle, buffalo, etc., and the hollow wing and leg bones of large birds. Relics found in numerous camps of American Indians indicate the redskins practiced wildlife calling, particularly for turkeys and waterfowl, on a rather large scale. Most of the Indians' calls were made from hollow bones or pieces of cane.

Obviously these calls were effective, otherwise the Indians (who sometimes tended to be lazy) would not have taken the time and trouble to make them or to use them.

When I was a kid, one did not have to travel very far to get into some respectable rabbit and squirrel hunting. It was a matter of filling one's pockets with .22 shorts, lugging a bolt action single-shot rifle in one hand, and guiding the bike with the other hand as one peddled to the outskirts of town. The only game call we knew about in those days was the duck call.

Still in a rudimentary way we practiced a bastardized kind of calling to get game out into the open for a clean shot. The cottontail bounding down the wagon trail usually came to an abrupt stop at the sound of a shrill whistle. Some of us used whistles that just shrieked; others had police whistles. The shrill sounds stopped the bunnies, and they would look back with a sort of "what the hell was that?" pose. Pow! And the bunny rolled over kicking in the dust. Down in the woods we would note in which trees the squirrels were hiding. Then to get the animals to stick their heads in the clear, we would tap a pocket knife sharply against the gun stock.

In the true sense we were not game calling. We were making sounds so foreign that the game simply had to take another look to see what it was all about. And the kids those days were good enough shots to make the most of the animals' indiscretions. One can still do the same thing today to make rabbits and squirrels expose themselves for a few seconds. The only trouble is modern kids spend so much time gawking at television they are unskilled at taking advantage of these pauses with old-fashioned country snap-shooting.

Game calls were primarily devised to aid the hunter to put meat on the table, and until recent years this was the sole role these calls played. Interest in our environment due mainly to widespread publicity given to vanishing and threatened species of wildlife has brought game calls into new hands, the hands of naturalists, photographers, and just plain amateur game and bird watchers. The calls are being used to bring wilderness creatures nearer for close observation and nature studies. I know scores of folks who would never squeeze a gun trigger on a bird or animal, yet they regularly go afield to use wildlife calls. This game calling is no passing fancy; it is here to stay. In this connection one chapter in this book is devoted to game and bird photography.

2.

Locate and Attract

THE FUNCTION OF THE WILDLIFE CALL IS TO ATTRACT AND/OR locate game. It becomes an attraction call when it lures the game to the user. It is a location call when the game sought responds only by answering back. In one case the call brings the game to the hunter; in the other it points the hunter in the direction of the game.

Needless to say the call that attracts eliminates hunter error in stalking and is the most effective. All the hunter need do is remain hidden and reasonably still. The game comes to him provided, of course, he uses the call properly.

With the call that locates the game but does not bring it in, the hunter has little margin for error. He sounds his call and gets an answer from across the meadow, on the other side of the stream, or up on the hillside. He can not be certain whether the game is 200 or 300 yards away. In the case of birdlife the situation is further complicated since the hunter does not know if the bird is on the ground or up in a tree—or for that matter which tree.

This location call gives the huntsman the knowledge that the game sought is in the immediate area and it points out its general location. It is up to the hunter to stalk the target, make visual contact, and then ease into effective gun range. It is no easy job even for an experienced stalker. It is a lost cause for the heavy-footed fellow who snaps a twig at every other step and rustles the branches of every bush he passes.

With some species of game the location call can be a valuable instrument. For example, consider quail hunting. This fine game-bird allows hunters to approach within a few feet. You can walk right up to these little fellows and often must kick the cover to make the birds flush. Even though quail are hunted with dogs that find the birds by scent, a quail call can be invaluable in first-time hunting a new field. An answer to your call will let you know whether or not birds are present in the field. Then it is a case of letting the dogs take it from there.

I have hunted quail sans dog and with quail whistle alone. The whistle aids in getting the general location of the birds, but it does not pinpoint them. Unless cover is so sparse that you can stalk each individual bush, quail hunting without a dog is strictly for the birds. In dense cover you can pass a covey by 15 feet without seeing a thing.

Another species that can be located by a call is the mourning dove. In this case the call can be most helpful in hunting a wooded area. Doves will answer the call. Then it is up to the hunter to home in on the direction of the response. At least it is easier than quail tracking. Doves make their presence known earlier by flying, and one can spot their movements in the trees. The dove coo is of some help in open fields where vegetation stands several feet high. The doves will be feeding on the ground, and their answers to your calls will head you in the right direction. Don't worry about passing them by. They are not like the quail that stay frozen in one place. Doves are likely to flush when the hunter is around 30 to 35 yards away. This is a very sporty in-range shot.

But don't get out in a field and sound either a quail or dove call and expect the birds to come to you. You will find this pretty fruitless hunting. It is possible to call in a few quail—singles that have been broken from covies—if you happen to be good with a quail whistle. The trouble is not many users are that proficient.

The call that only locates the game is fine if the user does not try to use it beyond its capabilities. Otherwise it can be like the rubber band that is stretched beyond its limits. It just won't work.

The attraction call is sounded much more frequently than the location call, but care must be exercised in not overdoing it. Always remember that the more the call is sounded, the more you are apt to blow sour notes.

How often you need to sound the attraction call is easy when the game sought is visible. When the game starts working to you, you ease off on the calling. But if the game shows signs of losing interest, you start calling again with vigor to recapture its attention.

It is far different in calling up unseen game, especially when it comes to varmints and predators. Suppose you are hunting coyote. In this case you will be using a call that makes a squeal like that of a wounded rabbit. These calls have considerable carry and a coyote a half-mile away may hear it. Unless you sound it often enough, the coyote will never come in close enough for a decent shot. The only thing the animal has to go on is its ears picking up the squeals you sound. It will take repeated calls to bring the beast in close. For this reason the hunter should sound his call at least a half hour in one place before moving to a new stand. Otherwise you may vacate a good spot before the game moves within range.

I recall one varmint hunt on which I noted a fox on the side of a mound a little more than a quarter-mile away. I had to get the animal in close because that day we were hunting with shotguns. The fellow with me did the calling, while I glassed the animal with binoculars. The fox showed no signs of hearing the sound until the third or fourth series of squeals. Then its ears went up, the animal stood up and started sniffing its nose in our direction. Fortunately the light breeze was perfect and the animal had no way of picking up our scent. It took a good 15 minutes of concentrated calling to get the fox to come down the mound and cross a little stream a hundred yards out. Then more insistent urging was needed to pull the critter into shotgun range.

Later that same morning another fox appeared on the side of the same hill. He responded quickly to the call and on the second or third squeal the animal broke into a fast trot in our direction. We had him in the bag within the space of a few minutes. I suppose the second animal was just hungrier than the first. Nevertheless it illustrates a point—do not expect every animal, even those of the same species, to act alike.

3.

Duck Calling

THE MOST POPULAR OF ALL CALLS IS THE DUCK CALL. EACH YEAR approximately two million waterfowlers purchase duck stamps. In over three decades of waterfowl hunting, I have run into an army of duck hunters, and I believe I could count on my fingers and toes the number of fellows who did not have duck calls. It seems to be a sort of status symbol in waterfowling. A fellow is just a nobody if he does not have a duck call hung around his neck or stashed in a jacket pocket. He may never use it, but he wants it to show because it stamps him as a duck hunter.

In the hands of an expert, a duck call is a deadly instrument. I have hunted with waterfowlers who were so skilled in calling that they called ducks within gun range without so much as a single decoy showing. Yet as universal and popular as this call is, only a small percentage of the overall total of hunters use it properly. Too many hunters use the duck call like hypochondriacs take aspirins. Instead of playing a tune for the ducks, they become too engrossed with entertaining themselves and their hunting pals. From the time they load their guns until they quit for the day, they call incessantly. The result is about the same as the Congressional filibuster.

It comes to a point where too much calling is worse than no calling at all. Wild animals and birds are far less chatterboxes than their domesticated counterparts. Walk into any barnyard and immediately the ducks and geese will start chattering. These same birds if they were in the wild would remain silent—and for a good reason. Every species of wildlife is preyed upon by other species, and survival is a matter of not attracting the attention of one's enemies. Consequently wildlife calls rather sparingly. Animals and birds are noisiest during the mating season, which is usually a closed season as far as the hunter is concerned.

A common fault of hunters calling ducks is to try to make the instrument perform beyond its limits. By this I mean the hunter sees a flock of ducks a half mile away and he blows himself blue in the face trying to attract the birds. If the wind is wrong, it is a cinch bet that the sound never reached the birds.

Experienced waterfowlers never bother with trying to turn any birds that may be more than several hundred yards away. Furthermore, they don't bother to call all birds that may fly within range of the sound. They are experienced to the degree to tell in a matter of seconds if the birds are flying because they are seeking new places to feed and rest or because they have had their tail feathers dusted with shot. They concentrate their calling on those birds that loaf along and meander. These are the birds that will respond most readily to good calling. Also, they don't bother to call huge flocks. They devote their attention to flocks numbering about a dozen and a half birds or less. The only time calling works to any degree of satisfaction on huge flocks is when the hunter likewise has a great number of decoys showing.

Unless a fellow is an expert with a call, he should limit its use to attracting the attention of the birds to his decoys. He should refrain from trying to "talk" them all the way to the water. The expert caller can do this, but the average hunter who attempts it is likely to spook the birds with false notes or too much calling.

The time to sound the call is when the birds are crossing in front of or to the side of the hunter or when they are going away. Never sound the call when the birds appear to be flying straight in. The hunter must keep in mind that these incoming birds are facing him, and it will be easy for them to pinpoint the source of the call. If they see the hunter or the hunter makes a foreign or sudden move, the birds are certain to vector away.

Sound the call when the birds are not looking in your direction. If you have to do any sounding at all when birds are facing you, it should be subdued feeding chuckles. And even then use these sparingly. The general rule of thumb is that the closer the ducks work, the less one sounds the call. There are three good reasons: (1) too much calling allows the ducks to pinpoint you, (2) the more one calls the greater the odds false notes will be sounded, and (3) the call is too loud.

With most game calls the purpose is to make one kind of sound and that is all. The duck call is an exception. There is an entire scale of calls that can be used, which include the hail, come on in, feeding chuckle, and come back. Actually the waterfowler can get by very well if he learns to master the hail call and feeding chuckle. These are the most consistent producers. Incidentally, all of these calls can be sounded on the same instrument. It is all a matter of cadence and volume used.

The hail call is the first to use. Its purpose is to attract the attention of passing ducks. It is a rather loud call that goes: "Ka-kaaack, kack, kack, kack, kack, kack." The initial "ka-kaaack, kack" is loud and drawn out. Succeeding "kacks" are shorter and decrease in volume. The sequence is repeated three or four times in succession with a pause of several seconds between calls. It should only be used when the ducks are crossing or angling away from the hunter. When the birds vector toward the hunter, switch over to the come on in call. This is a series of two or three "kack, kack, kacks," with a pause of a second or two between each "kack," that should express contentment. It is a call with moderate volume initially, and it is decreased as the ducks come closer.

The feeding chuckle need not be used if the birds show definite signs in working to the decoys. Use the feeding chuckle when the birds appear undecided and begin to waver off. The feeding chuckle is quite easy to sound. One simply says: "tic-a-tic-a-tic-a-tic-a-tic" rapidly into the call. Since it is a chuckle, there is no need for any great volume. The feeding chuckle can be spiced up and made even more alluring with an occasional "kack" or two interspersed. Be sure to pause several seconds between chuckles. Don't make a continuous sonata.

The really important thing about calling ducks, particularly when decoys are used, is to shut up completely when the birds set their wings. I have seen many hunters completely spook birds by insisting on giving one last little call when the birds are gliding down. I have been guilty of it, and it is something one learns only through experience.

The come back call is used only when the birds veer off and seem bent on heading for the horizon. It is similar to the hail call but with a lot of pleading. The individual "kacks" are stretched out to longer "kaaacks" and constant volume is maintained throughout the entire sequence. Don't be disappointed if it fails to turn the birds, for it is the least effective of all calls.

The various calls needed to attract ducks can be learned from records, and there are a number of these on the market. However, I have yet to find a record with what I call the talk back call. This is a call I picked up from hunting guides, and probably the reason it is not on records is because it varies so greatly.

This talk back call is a deadly one to use on singles and doubles. It is nothing more than an imitation of what the flying duck is saying, and it can be learned only when the waterfowler trains himself to listen for duck sounds. It is a subdued, soft call that can be completely missed if the hunter fails to remain alert. The call invariably comes from ducks bent on decoying but undecided as to which pond they want to visit. When the flying duck talks, immediately answer it in kind with a carbon copy call, but be sure it is soft and subdued. Don't go into a sequence of calls. Simply answer the duck and shut up until it makes another sound and then answer this in kind.

The sound made by the conventional duck call imitates the hens of the species. Drakes from species to species make sounds other than the standard "kack." For example, the drake mallard makes a call that sounds like a low-pitched "creep" rather than an outright "kack." Drake mallard calls are made, but relatively few are in use for they have such limited range. The drake pintail whistles instead of "kacks." A number of calls are made to imitate this sound, and they are usually referred to as "sprig whistles."

The standard duck call, the one that imitates the hens, will attract almost all species of ducks, puddlers as well as divers. The skilled caller regulates call cadence and volume to fit the species of birds most predominant in an area. He sounds "kacks" in the call to attract the puddler ducks such as mallards, pintails, teal, black ducks, gadwalls, etc. He sounds a "brrrr-r-r-r-r" in the call for the popular species of diving ducks such as canvasbacks, redheads, and scaup. The "brrrr-r-r-r-r" sounded for the canvasback is deep and throaty; for the scaup and redhead it is higher pitched, shorter, and crisper.

Unless one gets moisture or dirt in the instrument, there is little likelihood of sounding any false notes on the "brrrr-r-r-r-r" for scaup and redheads. Both of these species respond extremely well to calling when it is used in conjunction with decoys. The mallard is one species that can be lured in by calling alone and with no decoys showing. But it takes an expert to do it. Even then they don't call the ducks expecting them to settle on the pond. The call is simply a means to turn the birds and get them to fly within effective gun range.

Some makes of duck calls have more reach than others, but this is not something that can be determined in the sporting goods store or in your living room. Reach or range can only be determined on the bayshore, on the lake, or in the marsh. I carry three duck calls. In the basement where I do a lot of my practicing they all sound pretty much alike. Yet out in the field one can be heard from a half-mile away, while the reach of the other two is less than a quarter-mile. On a blustery day when there are a lot of covering sounds from breaking waves and rustling marsh vegetation, the call with the half-mile reach is ideal. It won't reach that far under these noisy wind conditions, but it reaches far enough to be heard and to be effective. This same call, however, is poor for hunting on a dead calm day. The "kacks" are right but they are far too loud and can spook birds that may be nearby. The other two calls with far less reach are ideally suited for no-wind-no-noise days.

Ducks and geese are waterfowl, but in respects to making sounds they have habits as different as night and day. Geese do all their calling while in flight. On the ground they are almost silent except for feeding chuckles that can be heard from only a short distance. Any time you hear geese loudly calling on the ground, you can bet the birds have been alarmed to a point just a fraction short of skeedaddling for more placid surroundings. Yet it is interesting to note that flying geese will respond to calls that emanate from the ground.

Ducks on the wing, however, are pretty much silent, When they do resort to talking it is when they are over other ducks on the water. Even then the talk is quite subdued. Drake mallards will speak out "creep, creep, creep," with a second or two pause between each individual "creep." The hen mallard will sound a subdued "kack." Drake pintails and baldpates will occasionally emit a low whistle. These same ducks on the water will become as talkative as the folks at the weekly bridge party. You will hear a wide assortment of "kacks," "creeps," whistles, and feeding chuckles.

Alarmed ducks just before taking to wing are as silent as a graveyard. Yet the second they leap into the air, there is another wide assortment of sounds with the raucous and drawn out "kaaack, kaaack, kaaack" of the hens drowning out the calls of the drakes.

It is important for the waterfowl caller to know these sounds, for the knowledge can save a lot of wear and tear on his lungs. It is absolutely useless and a complete waste of time to call ducks when they are sounding the alarm call. This also holds true in attempting to call geese that have just taken off in alarm.

The duck call is an instrument used in weather extremes, and it takes a beating from the elements. It is a hardy instrument, but it can be damaged badly, even ruined, in fumbling and incompetent hands. For a reason I have yet to determine, a great many fellows puff a duck call a few times in the sporting goods store, buy it, and then as soon as they get home, take—or attempt to take—it apart. A few models screw together, but in the case of most, the mouthpiece end is wedged into the trumpet end. If the call is well made, it takes some muscle to pull the two apart. Yet many fellows will take a pencil or some blunt instrument, insert it in the trumpet end, and then drive out the mouthpiece by hammering on it. If they are lucky, they will miss hitting the reed. Most are not that lucky, and a damaged reed will completely change the pitch and sound of the call.

A duck call—or for that matter any call—should not be tampered with unless it becomes inoperable. Leave well enough alone.

4.

Calling Geese

OUR SPREAD OF DECOYS HAD BEEN OUT IN THE RICE STUBBLE FOR more than an hour, and although a few geese were flying, not a single bird had moved within a quarter-mile of our rig. The hunt had all the makings of one of *those* days.

And then the weather that had been building up in the northeast started piling in our direction. The wind picked up and with it came pelting, stinging rain. Had the birds been working my hunting partner and I would have stayed out in the weather, but since the skies were almost sterile of geese, we vacated the blind to take shelter behind a small levee and got under some overhanging brush. Our decision was to pick up the decoys and quit as soon as the driving rain let up.

We were able to keep remarkably dry and comfortable under the brush, and to while away the time I got to playing with a Hotchkiss goose call. The instrument was made like a turkey call—cedar box with hinged lid that produced the goose "galoop, galoop" when stroked lightly over a piece of slate. I liked the call because it produced an excellent imitation of the cry of the snow and blue goose, but I was telling my companion, W. J. Stines, Jr., that I didn't think much of it otherwise for it had little reach or range.

"I don't think this thing can be heard a hundred yards away," I remarked. "Still it sure makes a beautiful sound."

I played with it for a time. Then Stines took his turn with it, and finally it came back to me again. We were not trying to call geese; we were simply playing to pass the time until the rain subsided.

And then right after a long series of "galoops" there came an

24

answer—and from real, real close. We both grabbed our guns with as little commotion as possible and peeked through the brush. Stines scanned the sky to his left; I eyeballed the heavens to the right. Nothing—not even a black bird flying.

"Give another little call," Stines urged.

I did, and again we got an answer. This time the answer clued us in that the reply came from on the ground.

"Damned thing must have lit in the decoys," Stines opined as he craned his neck to check over the rig. "We'll have to climb over the levee to see the decoys and they're out of gun range. Bird probably lit on the far side and with so little cover we never could sneak up close enough for a shot. Keep calling. Let's see what happens."

So I returned to urging with the call and after each one I got an answer. Only now it was obvious the answer was moving—moving toward us.

"Keep calling," Stines whispered. "That goose has got to show itself some place."

More urging with the call, and more answers. Each time seemingly a little closer. We were as nervous as two kids sneaking into a watermelon patch. From the volume of the answers the bird had to be in gun range. But where was it?

Then suddenly Stines eased back down from the levee. He crawled about 20 feet to his right where the levee angled back toward the field. When he got to the corner, he peered around cautiously. I heard a faint "snick" as he released the safety on his gun. Then he stepped quickly around the corner and then "blam!" Naturally I hustled over, and there not more than 25 feet from him lay a headless blue goose. The range was too close for the shot to spread, so rather than tear up the bird with a body shot, Stines simply fired for the head.

Personally I don't think my calling had a thing to do with getting the bird out of the sky. I doubt if it even heard the call. It simply saw our decoys on the ground and came down to the spread. The decoys were about 70 yards from the shelter we had sought, and I'm certain that once the bird was on the ground, it heard my call and answered. I think perhaps more out of curiosity than anything else, the bird waddled around seeking out the source. I honestly believe that had I called long enough the bird would have rounded that bend in the levee and come to us face to face.

The goose call is like the duck call in that it attracts the game to the hunter. It works best when used in conjunction with decoys. The call catches the attention of the birds. They then see the decoys, and if everything looks right they drop in for a visit. Geese like ducks can be called in with absolutely no decoys showing, but in this situation geese are considerably less responsive.

There are, however, major differences between goose and duck calling. With a duck call it is useless to attempt to turn birds a quarter-mile away. Not so with geese. If you have a call with the volume, you can attract geese a half-mile off. One false note with a duck call, and you can spook the flock. No need to worry about "falsettos" with a goose call. The reason here is that the notes you feel are false are also darned good imitations of the cries made by juvenile geese. And believe me, immature geese can make some of the weirdest sounds.

The key to good goose hunting is a good show of decoys. Yet a fellow active with his call and with just a handful of decoys can take 75 percent of the play away from the fellow with a big decoy rig but no call. Geese are just that way. They love conversation. As long as there are a few decoys showing, they will respond to calling. This is especially so if snow and blue geese are involved.

One point must be made clear in calling geese. They respond when they are flying. You're wasting lung power trying to get a flock to leave the ground in response to your call. This can be done readily with ducks but not with geese.

A good goose call must have volume. It must be one that can be heard a half-mile away. I love waterfowl hunting and have been doing it for more than 30 years. Occasionally I get on a "specialty" kick. I had such a kick back in the early 1950s when for three seasons straight I hunted strictly for snow and blue geese. Time after time my calling caught the attention of birds a good half-mile off and turned them 90 degrees to home in on my spread of decoys. On several occasions I had small going-away gaggles do a 180-degree turn to visit the decoys.

The secret in calling a distant gaggle of geese is to make a lot of noise. Call constantly, pausing only to get a fresh supply of air in your lungs. When the birds turn in your direction, get just a little frantic in your calling. Then after they appear to have their minds set on visiting your area, begin toning down on the call. When they are about 200 yards out be sure to decrease volume for you don't want the call to sound like a bugle blast.

If the geese are snows or blues, you can keep working the call until a few seconds before you shoot. With speckled-belly or white-fronted geese it is best to shut up when they are still about 100 yards out. These geese are much warier than snows and blues, and if they spot you—the hunter—they are sure to vector off. They are great at pinpointing the exact location of the call.

When Canada geese, or any of the Canada sub-species, are involved, stop the talk when the birds are 150 to 200 yards off, for they are even warier than the speckled-bellies. However, with Canadas one must take in a characteristic of the species. Prior to decoying these birds will case the area thoroughly. This means they may make several wide and meandering circles around the area before turning to the decoys. When the birds begin to move away in starting this circle, the hunter should resume calling to keep the birds' minds on the decoys. There is a complication that must be considered. Always remember there may be a guy in the next field, and he might by trying to work the same gaggle.

The main geese hunted in North America include snow, blue, speckled-belly, and Canada and its sub-species. Each main species has a distinct call.

The snows and blues are the noisiest of the lot. Their basic call is a "galoop, galoop, galoop." The cry of the snow is a bit higher pitched and shriller than that of the blue goose. This really presents no problem since snows and blues will respond to each other's calls. Furthermore, they readily mix and fly together on wintering grounds.

The speckled-belly's cry is a medium-pitched "galooping" yodel. The sound can be produced by fluttering one's tongue when blowing the call, or by blowing steady and then making the yodel by alternately cupping and opening one's hand over the trumpet end of the call. It is not an easy call to produce with the standard call, and if the hunter specifically seeks speckled-belly geese, he should purchase a call designed expressly for this species. Fortunately for Mr. Average Hunter, speckled-belly geese will respond reasonably well to snow and blue goose calls if there is a good show of decoys.

The Canada goose's call is a deep resonant "he-ronk, he-ronk, he-ronk." The Canada's sub-species, which are birds smaller in size, make the same cry except somewhat higher pitched. Although Canadas will occasionally angle to decoy rigs spiced with snow, blue, or speckled-belly calling, it is far better to go with a call specifically designed for attracting the majestic honker.

The goose call in comparison with the duck call is a delicate instrument. You can get it out of whack quickly by taking it apart and attempting to tamper with its innards. It must also be protected from undue moisture. A wet goose call produces sounds akin to a raccoon's fight squall, and since the raccoon is one of the goose's deadliest enemies, it goes without saying the coon sounds will send geese winging to the horizon.

Although the goose call is mainly an attraction call, it serves as an excellent game locator in one instance. Far more geese are knocked down as cripples than as clean kills. A wing-clipped goose can volplane and go down in the marsh or prairie a quarter-mile from the hunter. True hunters who know the value of conservation make an honest effort to recover these birds, but recovery is often most difficult. If there are any weeds at all the bird will hide. The bird can hunker down in cover, and you can walk within feet of it and never see it. This is where the goose call comes into play. If you fail to find the bird, move a little distance away from where you feel the bird may be hiding and wait five or ten minutes. This is usually enough time for the bird to overcome most of its initial fright.

Then start with the goose call, using the long, drawn out forlorn call of the typical lost goose. If the downed bird is sufficiently over its fright, it will answer. Remember these birds are gregarious and not loners. They keenly desire the company of other geese. Keep calling as you work toward the spot from which the answers appear to come. In nine cases out of ten the bird will usually stretch its head high to locate the call, and often will be within range of the "cripple-stopper" shot, which is nothing more than a shell loaded with small shot—6 or 7½ size. Shot this small will not bring down a flying goose, for at long range the bird's heavy feathers will turn the shot. Usually "cripple-stopper" shots on the ground are at ranges of about 30 to 35 yards with the goose just sticking its head above the cover. That head and neck does not present much of a target, and you need a dense shot pattern to register a hit. The loads charged with 6 or 7½ size shot are ideal for this situation.

5.

Squirrel Calling

HIGH NOON ON A HOT, WINDLESS DAY IS NOT THE TIME TO HUNT squirrels. We should have been deep in the woods hunting the bushy-tails very early that morning, and we would have, too, had it not been for a faulty water pump on the way up. The guy at the roadside auto repair shop did good work and was fair enough on his prices, but his working speed was dead slow.

Still, we were here in an East Texas woods and we had come to hunt squirrels and squirrels we were going to hunt. Even if the time of day was wrong we had along an instrument in which we placed implicit faith. It had worked many times before, and there was no reason why it could fail this time. Unless, of course, the woods were sterile of squirrels.

The instrument was a squirrel call, a gadget that if used properly will get you bushy-tails every time—if you can hit the animals when you see them.

We saw signs where squirrels had been recently, but as far as the animals themselves we saw not a flicker. My partner and I found comfortable spots on opposite sides of a large oak tree. Then my partner fished his squirrel call out of his pocket. His was a neat little gadget with a large ring. He slipped the ring over the middle finger of his left hand and operated the call by rapidly squeezing the attached rubber ball. It produced the "kuk-kuk-kuk-kuk-kuk" bark of a squirrel. He started his calling gently—a few light "kuks" and then silence.

Gradually he picked up the tempo until about ten minutes later he had a lively chatter going. It was then that we began to hear a few barks in return. All the while we were as motionless as tombstones, and in our camouflage suits we looked a part of the woods. All we moved were our eyes, scanning the adjacent trees for squirrel signs. My buddy continued his calling, imitating the rapid-fire chatter of a squirrel that had just found the nut cache of all times. Meanwhile the tempo of the barks in return picked up, and to make things more interesting they came from different directions. Obviously the calling was stirring bushy-tails out of their midday siestas and from the sound of things we had at least two, maybe more, heading in our direction.

And then I saw movement high in a tree to my right. On an ordinary day I would not have seen the movement, but this day there was absolutely no wind and something very much alive had to be shaking that tree limb. Suddenly there was a blur of gray as the squirrel leaped to the limb of an adjacent tree, and at almost the same time another ball of fur came running down a tree trunk dead ahead. To make a long story short we got both animals within easy shotgun range—and had two squirrels in the bag. In the next two hours we dropped three more. In each case the animals came to the call. Had we been hunting without a call, I doubt seriously if we would have even seen a single bushy-tail. It was just the wrong time of the day for them to stir around on their own. Something had to arouse and stimulate their interest. My partner's expert use of his squirrel call did just that.

The most effective squirrel calls are those that are hand operated. The call is held in the web between the thumb and forefinger in such a manner that the bellows, usually just a rubber bulb, points up. Then with the extended fingers on his other hand, the hunter sharply taps the bellows or bulb. The sound produced is the "kuk" bark of a squirrel. You can regulate the pitch by closing down the fingers holding the call. Pitch is important on a quiet, windless day for you don't want the sound to be like that of a small dog.

I have found that on a windy day, however, the call can be reversed in one's hand and operated by one hand alone. In this case the bellows is held inside the palm of the hand. The operation then is to tap the bellows sharply against the side of your leg. The bark will be louder than when the fingers are closed around the mouth of the call, but in this case the extra volume is necessary in order to be heard above the wind and rustling of leaves and limbs.

There are two kinds of calls to sound. These are usually referred to as the "anger" call and the "contented" call. There is a time for each as well as a time for a combination of the two.

The "anger" call is most effective early in the season, and it imitates the strident bark of an angry or belligerent squirrel. Master this call and you can get the bushy-tails to come right to you.

Here is how the call goes. Tap the instrument sharply three or four times. This produces the sharp "kuk, kuk, kuk," which is the first part of the call. Then tap the call very, very rapidly to produce a continuous and machine gun-like "kukkukkukkukkuk-kukkuk." This is the second part of the call. Now put the two together, and you get a sound like this: "kuk kuk kuk kuk kuk-kukkukkukkukkukkuk." Sound this call once, twice at the most. Then maintain a silence of perhaps a half minute before repeating it. If there is a squirrel around to take up the challenge, the animal will do so in short order. When you hear this challenge, immediately answer with your challenge. These animals have their own territories, and they resent outside squirrels intruding.

This call becomes less effective as the season progresses, especially in woods that are hunted frequently. Then the animals are wary and suspicious, and they will approach this call with stealth. They will sneak in quietly and slowly, and if they happen to spot you, they will vanish the same way they came. The squirrel learns quickly that man is a threat.

When the bushy-tails are wary, the sound to make is that of the contented squirrel, the squirrel that is telling its kin that all is well in the woods. The sound, of course, must be soft, and it is produced by a series of gentle taps on the bellows of the instrument. It goes like this: "kuk kuk kuk kuk kuk, kuk-kuk, kuk, kuk, kuk." Make this sound a half dozen or so times with a pause of 15 to 30 seconds between calls. Meanwhile keep your eyes on the trees. This call will not only bring the animals down to join in the fun, but it will also lure in those crusty old individuals bent on a challenge or argument.

Combining the "anger" call with the "contented" call is a good way to stir squirrels in a woods that has been hunted moderately heavy. The "anger" call is sounded first. Use it three or four times. This is to attract attention and alert any nearby animals that something is happening. Then pause and follow up with a series of "contented" calls. This combination will arouse curiosity in the soul of even a recently shot at squirrel.

Now in all squirrel calling hunter immobility is an absolute must. It goes without saying that your clothing must blend in with the woods. You can't walk around using a squirrel call and expect to get results. After you locate the animals with your call, then you can stalk around the tree in which they are located in order to catch them in the open. But first use the call to determine their exact location before making any unnecessary moves. And remember when you do move, go slow and easy.

Many years ago a guide taught me a trick to use to get a treed squirrel to expose itself. It is most exasperating to find a tree with a squirrel and then never get the animal to expose itself enough for a decent shot. As you stalk around the tree, the squirrel will do the same thing, always keeping the trunk or limb between itself and you. All you see is an eye and an ear, and maybe the flick of a tail. None of this makes a shootable target unless you're hunting with a shotgun, and even with the scatter-gun results are doubtful with a target so small. So here is where the guide's trick comes into the act.

Carry a paper sack with a half dozen whole pecans plus a few broken shells. Now let's carry this through a typical situation. You have located the critter and circled the tree a half dozen times, but the animal always manages to keep hidden. Leave the tree and move to a nearby one and get behind it in such a way so that you can watch the tree with the squirrel but still keep most of your person hidden from the animal. Now gently shake the paper sack with the pecans. Do it timidly at first and then slowly pick up the tempo. Unless the squirrel is badly frightened, it will stick up its head offering you a clear, clean shot.

The guide who taught me the trick said the pecans rattled in the bag are exactly like the sounds made by a squirrel rustling with a cache of nuts in dry leaves around the base of a tree. The trick has worked too many times for me to knock it.

I have found that the pecan rattling plus a few contented "kuk kuk kuk kuk-kuk kuk kuks" on the squirrel call can stimulate the animals ever quicker.

Where you find squirrels you will also find woodpeckers and blue jays. One can be used to your advantage; the other can royally foul up the works.

A woodpecker drilling away on a dead tree can be a big help to the squirrel hunter. The bird's snare-drumming seems to give the bushy-tails a sense of security. They hear the pecker's racket and come out of hiding to carry on their every day chores. Tyro game callers object to other noises in the area when they sound their calls. They feel any additional noises are competition. In reality the other noises, like the drilling of the woodpecker as an example, lend authenticity to the scene.

There are some woods noises that will cancel out the effectiveness of the game call. There is not much a fellow can do about wind or rain. One just has to make the best of these natural cause situations and try to beat them by increasing call volume. Now consider the blue jay. This bird is one that often sends all wildlife scurrying for cover. This bird seems to have a sixth sense that enables it to detect danger, and when the blue jay does, it vocalizes its feelings with the result being that everything around takes off for cover. If your squirrel call is getting competition from a blue jay, you can figure you have had it. You can shoot the bird if it is not protected by law. A more sensible solution is simply to stop all calling, settle down and become as motionless as possible. The bird will lose interest in you in five or ten minutes and then wing away to another part of the woods. But if you keep active and moving around, the blasted jay will hang in the vicinity for hours.

6.

The Turkey Call

THE SUREST WAY OF GETTING A WILD TURKEY IS TO HUNT WITH A turkey call. Scouring the woods for turkey without a call is like trying to propel a battleship with a pair of oars. You may see plenty of turkey signs, hear them elsewhere in the woods, but as far as visual contact is concerned, there will be mighty little.

The turkey undoubtedly has the keenest eyesight of all inhabitants of the forest. It notes every little movement, and if the movement is the least bit out of character, Tom and his hens skeedaddle. This is exactly what happens with the hunter who aimlessly meanders the forests searching out the birds. He can consider himself extremely fortunate if he rounds a bend and finds these magnificent birds in a spot offering a clear shot. If he is quick and able to pick out a legal bird, he might be able to get off one hasty shot. Even then it is likely to be a haphazard one, and you know the results of hasty shooting—a clean miss or a hit in a spot that tears up good table meat.

And then, of course, the flock scatters. Fortunately for the hunter the flock tends to scatter much like a covey of quail breaks. They head out in various directions away from the hunter. If they flushed and all headed off in the same direction like a drove of ducks, the hunter would be in a pickle. The turkey flock immediately scatters, but again fortunately for the hunter, the birds don't travel great distances. Usually it is not more than several hundred yards. Almost immediately the scattered birds will yelp, cluck, and whine in an effort to reassemble. Turkeys are gregarious birds. They love company, and a single bird will not remain separated long from its kinsmen.

This is where the turkey call comes into play, and if the user is skilled, the instrument is almost a sure guarantee of a bird in the bag. With judicious calling the hunter can bring individual birds back to an assembly point. But he must be good with the call, for the simple reason his call will be in direct competition with real "turkey talk" from other members of the flock. The fellow who can whip this competition is a real artist with the call. The hunter who is just average in calling skill will pull in birds, but most likely they will be young immature ones not yet wise to survival in the wild.

There are only a few words in a turkey's vocabulary, but as in duck calling each word or sequence of words has a special meaning. There is the cluck of the gobbler and the cluck of the hen. If a hen is sought, then the hen cluck must be sounded. Except during the mating season, toms will ignore hen clucks. The gobbler, however, in the winter months will answer to the gobbler cluck.

Unfortunately for the hunter, turkey language contains two words sounding very much alike. One is a "cluck," the other is a "putt." The fellow who gets his "clucks" and "putts" mixed up is in for real trouble. The hunter who is attempting to "cluck" the scattered birds back together has had it if he slips in a "putt." The "putt" happens to be the turkey alarm call, and this is the call that will run game off. Obviously a good caller must keep his mind on what he is trying to do, and he must have a pretty good ear for music.

What holds true for the "cluck" and "putt" also holds true for the different "yelps." If one is to be successful with the turkey call, he must know the hen "yelp," the gobbler "yelp," and the hen's love "yelp" that is sounded so frequently during the spring mating season.

The best way to learn effective turkey calling is to take in-structions from an expert and then practice long hours, purchase a turkey call record and practice long hours, or get into the wild and listen to wild turkey talk and then practice more long hours. The record method is the quickest and easiest, and in the space of a few weeks of conscientious and intent practice a fellow can master the art sufficiently to produce satisfying results in the woods. The nice thing about the turkey call is that once you master the technique and the various calls, you will not forget them—certainly not after all those long hours of practice. A fellow can learn to blow a varmint call in a half hour, and then he can go out and get some results. You can not do this with a turkey call. You must get the various calls down pat, as there is no room for a single sour note.

In this respect the turkey caller must always be on guard not to overdo his calling, for the more the calling the greater the odds of sounding a falsetto. Call the birds. When they start talking, talk the same language back to them, but don't try to get fancy or attempt to add any embellishments of your own. Always keep in mind that you are dealing with a highly suspicious bird. It will rarely respond to a call at a trot the way a fox homes in on a varmint call. Instead the turkey will "cluck" or "yelp" and take a few steps. It will stand still, head raised to eye everything in sight. Another "cluck" or "yelp," a few steps forward, and another pause to eyeball the surroundings.

It is both irritating and exhilarating to spot a responsive tom or hen just out of gun range or on the other side of thicket too dense to shoot through. You call and the bird answers. It moves a little, then stops and calls again. You answer. This goes on and on like a broken record. It is quite common for a hunter to work a single bird for 10 or 15 minutes to get in decent position for an effective shot.

To make the sport even more intriguing is the fact that birds do not answer to the same calls day in and day out. One day they may respond to "clucks" and ignore "yelps." The next day it may be vice versa. It is up to the caller to try both calls and then stick with the one that draws answers. All the while he must be on guard so as not to inject an inadvertent "putt" that will turn the birds away. In this respect, it behooves the caller to first use the "yelp" to gain attention. Go to the "cluck" when all else fails, but keep your mind on what you are doing because if a single "putt" slips in, you will turn the birds away.

All that has been written so far concerns calling in birds that have just been scattered from the flock. The birds that will answer the quickest and return the fastest will be the young ones, particularly the hens. Those old toms are slow in answering and returning. Remember they got to be old birds by being all cautious. The only time toms respond rapidly is during the spring mating season. At this time of the season survival is not number one in their little minds.

There are times when calling will get birds to come in on the run. This occurs when they have been separated a long time from the flock. It seems they just want the company of another turkey, so the heck with caution and in they come on a dead run. And they usually come in yelping at almost every step.

Some turkey calls are blown; others are hand operated. It would be unfair to say one is superior to the other. It is a matter of personal choice and dexterity of operation on the part of the user. I know expert duck callers who can't blow a mouth-operated turkey call worth a hoot. Yet they get fine results with the hand-operated box call. Each call has its advantages and disadvantages. For example, false notes are likely with the blown call if the user is tired and winded from a long trudge through the woods. In this case he would be better off with a hand box call. This hand call, too, has its drawbacks. The most noticeable will be in damp weather when moisture is likely to result in either a squeal or rasp when the call is operated. Consequently in wet weather the hunter may be better off with a blown call.

There are a number of battery-operated electronic turkey calls on the market. All I have used or heard produced authentic sounds. Still I know a number of good turkey hunters who prefer the mouth- or hand-operated calls to the electronic devices.

In regard to electronic calls I must relate a particular hunt on which such a call was employed. It occurred in the Texas Hill Country, which is the heart of turkey hunting in Texas. The fellow who owned the call played it all morning, but it brought in no birds. That same afternoon and in the same area four other hunters using hand box calls lured in and bagged three gobblers. I can only assume that like so many electronic gadgets, the turkey record was used so indiscriminately that it may have repelled birds rather than attracted them. The fault, I believe, rested solely on the shoulders of the user. He became so imbued with the wonderful sounds intoned that he forgot the habits of the game he sought. The hunter spent his time just making a lot of noise.

The turkey call is one that may attract game other than turkeys, even in areas where the turkey population is quite heavy.

I recall a deer hunt on which a member of our party decided to concentrate on gobblers more than bucks. He used an electronic call. The night before our hunt he slipped out and put the device into operation behind the cabin. The resulting sounds broke up a poker game and elbow-bending session. The next morning he set up in a draw that was known to be frequented by turkeys. Throughout the morning the rest of us were in our deer blinds. We could hear the wonderful turkey calls produced by our companion's instrument, and we heard considerable shooting. Personally I had visions of the fellow being either a horrible shot or shooting way over the legal limit.

The rancher picked us up about noon in his truck. The last stop was the turkey stand, and I was wondering what the rancher's reaction would be if he found our buddy-boy surrounded with a half dozen dead turkeys. He certainly did enough shooting to bag that many. As it turned out, our great turkey hunter had nary a bird. Instead he had a collection of three foxes and two coyotes. And he confessed to not so much as seeing a single turkey. The rancher was happy the fellow had pruned down the predator population, and I was happy our caller did not louse up a good hunting arrangement.

I have seen this same thing happen on subsequent hunts, and I have come to the conclusion that the turkey call is almost as good as the rabbit-in-agony screams for attracting predators. Also game other than varmints will home in on the turkey call. A number of turkey callers have had deer respond. The only explanation is that both turkeys and deer feed on mast, and that perhaps the deer hearing turkey noises simply associates the sounds with food. By the same token there are hunters who have had turkeys respond to deer calls.

7

Varmint Calling

OUTDOOR WRITING HAS ITS REWARDS. WRITERS ARE EXTENDED ALL sorts of fishing and hunting invitations. They are bombarded also with new products and their accompanying news releases. If a writer is to keep abreast of the times, he must conscientiously field test products received. Some are not worth the material of which they are made, yet others are truly worthwhile gimmicks that can benefit the outdoorsman.

More years ago than I care to admit to, the U.S. mail brought me a package. The accompanying letter described the package contents—a fox call—as the ultimate for attracting foxes into gun range. And, of course, there were instructions on how to use the instrument.

Playing with outdoor gimmicks in a newspaper editorial room always draws co-workers like flies to carrion. I use the comparison because most creative writers and editors look down on outdoors writing as a necessary evil. The result is most editorial chiefs take delight in shooting arrows at the outdoor writer when he fiddles and faddles with a new product.

The outdoors scribe is supposed to be an expert in the use of any and everything remotely connected with the outdoors. He is supposed to operate the thing right the first time.

And so I sounded—or attempted to sound—the fox call. The resulting noise turned the newsroom into a hall of laughter—all derisive. The sound that came out of the instrument was quite like that of the play doll that cries "wa-wa-wa" when turned on its back. And this thing was supposed to call a fox? Immediately the newsroom attitude was one of "now go out and prove yourself as an outdoorsman."

Quite frankly I was sorry I ever opened the package at the

office. But as later events proved out, I am glad I did. Had I opened it at home and made that ridiculous baby crying wail, I might have tossed the instrument in a drawer and promptly erased it from memory like a bad dream. But now I was on the spot because defensively I had told co-workers it would work. During the next week the fellows, even a cub reporter, greeted me with: "Called any foxes lately?" Consequently my speaking too soon had fitted me into a shoe in which I had to walk or else.

I dug up an old hunting buddy—one that would not laugh—and got permission from a farmer to hunt his woods. The farmer had been the victim of several fox raids on his hen house, so he was willing to do almost anything to protect his stock.

We went about a quarter of a mile deep into the woods and took our stand under a huge magnolia tree. Out came the fox call, and I went to work with it in earnest. But, oh, that sound. My hunting companion did not laugh but he did comment: "You gotta be kidding." I sounded the thing off and on for a quarter of an hour. We saw a lot of game—blue jays flicking among the trees, a couple of woodpeckers atop a dead tree, and a squirrel. But we did not see a single fox.

"Well, let me give it another half hour," I said, "and if we don't get anything by then, we'll just forget it all and go hunt some squirrels."

And so I started wailing on the call again, but I must confess my heart was not in it. I was right on the verge of writing the instrument off as just another gadget designed to separate a gullible fellow from his money, when a small fox scurried into a clearing about a hundred feet in front of us. The animal did not sneak out of the brush. It came out in a rush. Its ears were erect and the hair on its collar bristled.

It was a distinct shock that anything should answer such a strange sounding call, and to make a long story short the two of us were so flabbergasted that we emptied our .22s at the animal with nary a hit. If anything, all the sand and dust kicked up by our errant bullets might have given the poor animal a lung infection. Nevertheless the experience gave us new founded faith in the call.

"Come on," my companion said. "Let's get deeper in the woods and give that damned call a real workout. It doesn't sound so crazy after all."

We trekked back into the woods and took turns playing the call with all the enthusiasm of the musician seeking to win the first chair in the orchestra. We called in and nailed four foxes. We also pulled a bobcat into sight briefly, but the animal also saw us and it made tracks fast.

The call I was using was labeled a fox call. Today the same call is being marketed as a varmint and predator call since experiences have proven it will lure a variety of game other than just the fox. I still have the call and occasionally use it. In addition to foxes, I have used it to bag coyotes, bobcats, coons, crows, and hawks.

A number of game species respond to the predator call. The list includes foxes, wolves, coyotes, raccoons, feral dogs, crows, and even the mountain lion. The easiest to call is the fox; the most difficult is the mountain lion or cougar. In fact, lion hunters I have talked to say the incident of a cougar responding to the call is rare even if the calling takes place in prime lion country. In each case that occurred the hunters were actually seeking foxes and coyotes when a lion chanced upon the scene. They also told me the cougars were immature yearlings. So for all practical purposes the hunter bent on a cougar would do far better hunting the animal in the conventional method using a pack of dogs.

The varmint call owner will get far more satisfactory results out of the instrument if he devotes his time to the species for which it was designed. These species are mainly three in number —fox, coyote, and wolf. In coon and bobcat country he will get only occasional response.

The fox is an extremely intelligent animal. Reynard can lead a pack of hounds a merry chase, and with its bag of tricks it can drive a poultry rancher to the brink of despair. It can live, propagate, and multiply in semi-urban areas without the people there ever realizing it. Yet it has one shortcoming that makes it a cinch for the varmint caller. The fox can not resist the wailing, terrorized cry of a crippled or trapped rabbit. Unless the animal has under gone the traumatic experience of several near hits from hunter's guns, the fox will throw caution to the wind and home in on the rabbit squeal like the forlorned desert wanderer reaches for the lake in the mirage.

Although foxes are nocturnal animals that do the bulk of their hunting at night, dawn, and dusk, a varmint caller can stir them out of their dens at midday. The animal can be called readily from a half-mile off. I know hunters who claim to have brought in foxes from distances as great as two miles. Although I have never been able to hear a varmint call past a half-mile, part of the scream may be at a decibel level that man can't hear. Perhaps it is like the "silent dog whistle." Then again the fox may just have ultra acute hearing. Regardless the reason, the varmint call is extremely effective where foxes are concerned.

The call to which Reynard responds can best be described as a combination scream, cry, wail, and whimper. The scream must be one of terror, the cry and wail must intone pain, and the whimper must have a distressing plea. The most effective call starts with the high-pitched scream, descends to the cry and wail, and ends with a "trailing off" whimper. Repeat the sequence two to four times, and then remain silent for a few minutes. Carry this out over a 15- to 20-minute period, and if you get no action, move to a new spot at least a half-mile away.

Always keep in mind that the fox, or for that matter all predators, hunt into the wind, depending mainly upon scent. The varmint caller is not appealing to scent. He makes his pitch to hearing, and this in turn plays to a basic weakness of the predators. They invariably respond quickly to the animal-in-distress call when the sound comes from an animal upon which they dine. And on the predators' menu the rabbit is filet mignon and caviar all rolled into one.

The normal fox approach is a trot. It will come in at a lope if the animal is particularly hungry or is in an area where competition for food is great. Often the creature will trot to within a few feet of the caller if the hunter is well hidden. A nervous fox will slow its approach when several hundred feet from the suspected source of the call. It will slink low to the ground and will generally quarter back and forth attempting to pick up scent. In heavy woods the animal is very likely to make a complete circle. Consequently, in areas where vision is limited it is advisable to hunt in pairs with one hunter watching to the front and the other to the rear. Believe me it is a heck of a shock to hear a sound behind, turn around, and stare eyeball to eyeball with a fox 10 or 15 feet away. When this happens it is a toss-up as to who suffers the worst fright—the hunter or the fox. There have been cases where incoming foxes actually collided with callers.

Although foxes generally hunt alone, the hunter in good fox country must be on the alert for the approach of more than one animal. I had one hunt when five foxes broke into the clearing in front of the blind at the same time. And they came from five different directions. The animals apparently were aware of each other and appeared to be racing to get to the rabbit first for they broke into the clearing on the dead run. The fact that my companion and I were using shotguns is the only reason the animals did not overrun our blind. We managed to drop three of the creatures before the other two took off into the brush.

After a fox has been bagged it is advisable to move to a new location unless you know for certain the place abounds with the beasts. I have been on hunts where as many as nine foxes were bagged from the same blind within a period of about three hours. Generally speaking, however, the average take at a location is two or three animals.

The same call sequence and techniques that bring in foxes will also produce results with coyotes and wolves. Coyotes can be called into easy gun range, or for that matter into bow and arrow range. Wolves, which are no longer as plentiful as they used to be, are very difficult to lure in close. Apparently they can pick up man's scent much easier than can either the fox or coyote.

Callers are apt to find coyotes working in pairs, and this can make the hunting tricky, for if one animal sights or scents the hunter, the beast will alert the other. If the animals have been hunted hard, there will be a flash of fur and the critters will vanish as if swallowed up by the earth.

Fortunately for the game callers, coyotes inhabit areas with far less cover and foilage than do foxes. This means the hunter can frequently see the coyote approaching from a considerable distance. Foxes are basically woods animals and do not like to take to open range unless forced to do so. Coyotes on the other hand avoid heavy woods. They can be called from far greater distances than foxes. The coyote like the fox will sometimes respond to the rabbit cry and whimper at midday.

Far greater results in varmint calling can be enjoyed by hunting at night when these animals are normally on the prowl. This kind of hunting must be done with one or more companions, for all 360 degrees of the compass must be watched. The same call sequence is used, but the hunting must be implemented with a strong spotlight. The method is to frequently pan the light beam around the area. The light should be directed toward the horizon with just fringe light, so to speak, falling to the ground. Eyes of the game will reflect like burning coals, and unless the light beam is directed right at the creatures they will not spook. If hunting in heavy timber, it pays to play the light well on the surrounding tree limbs where bobcats, racoons, and possums are likely to be. The bobcat responds to the call because it feeds on rabbits. The coons and possums put in their appearances more out of curiosity than anything else.

Approaching game, particularly large animals like coyotes, can be seen without aid of the light on bright moonlit nights in the desert or semi-arid regions. The light, however, is necessary to make positive target identification before shooting. Always keep in mind that the moving shape could be a ranch dog, domestic livestock, a deer, or maybe even another hunter.

Whether it is open country or deep woods, carefully check game laws on the use of spotlights. The mere fact that you have a spotlight and a gun in hand is in many areas "prima facia" evidence of spotlighting deer. This can be an expensive game regulation violation.

In spite of the fact that many varmint calls are described by their manufacturers as being effective for wolves, I doubt seriously that more than a handful of the big canines have met their doom as a result of wildlife calls. The main reason is that the wolf population, especially in the United States, is dreadfully low. The timber wolf (*canis lobo*), that brute made so vicious by storied tales, is found today only in a few of the states bordering Canada and in Canada itself.

Most states still have small populations of red wolves. Some are certainly lured to doom by varmint calls, but I can not help but feel that many of the so-called wolves bagged are canines that inexperienced hunters incorrectly identified. No doubt some of the animals with darkish coats were actually coyotes. If not, they were probably coy-dogs, a strain that results when a coyote mates with a dog. Coy-dogs are larger, bolder, and darker colored than true coyotes.

In order to distinguish a coy-dog from a coyote, certain mouth measurements are necessary. Measure the distance between the front of the first molar tooth to the back of the last molar in the animal's upper jaw. Then divide this figure by the distance across the roof of the mouth between the molars. A ration of 3.1 or more means the animal is a coyote. It is a coy-dog if the ratio falls between 2.7 and 3.1. If it is 2.7 or less, the animal is all dog.

An adult male coyote is about the size of an adult female red wolf. The coyote, however, will be a slender animal with small feet and narrow muzzle. In relation to a gray wolf, the coyote is much smaller. On the run, the coyote travels with its long tail held down. The wolf holds its tail high, even when moving full speed. The tracks, the howl, and the hide hold more positive clues to identification. Coyote tracks are small, while those of the wolf, even the small red wolf, are large. A coyote's howl is usually preceded by sharp barks, sometimes yaps. The wolf very rarely barks, but it makes long howls, often for hours on end. The coyote's hide is of poor quality in relation to that of a wolf. The hide of the coyote is papery and very thin. A wolf has a firm and heavy hide, much like calfskin.

An acquaintance who owns a large ranch used to have a large German shepherd that roamed the ranch at will. The ranch as well as several adjoining spreads had sizable fox populations plus a fair sprinkling of coyotes. And, of course, there were folks around who used varmint calls. To make a long story short, the German shepherd vanished and to this day the owner maintains the dog homed in on a varmint call and was shot for a wolf.

Probably a lot of other dogs, especially those with general wolfish profiles, have been shot by varmint callers. A lot of farm dogs vanish every year. These animals raised on the farms know and recognize the squeal of the distressed rabbit. Some probably have been fed rabbit meat by their owners. Consequently it is logical to assume that these dogs may have responded to some seductive varmint calling and in turn were shot by tyro hunters. This is the sort of thing that makes for poor farmer-hunter relations.

8.

Upland Game Birds

INDIVIDUAL CHAPTERS HAVE BEEN DEVOTED TO CALLING DUCKS, geese, turkeys, and crows simply because calls are used so frequently in hunting these species. Calls are also used in pheasant, chukar partridge, and quail hunting, but since hunters using calls for these species are in a minority, these birds will be dealt with in a single chapter. The long-established method of seeking these birds with dogs is so sporting and thrilling that I doubt if calls will ever really make serious inroads into pheasant, chukar, and quail hunting. All you have to do is hunt these fine game birds once with a good dog, and you will never hunt them any other way. A fine bird dog in action is a creature of real beauty.

But in the event you do not have a bird dog, let's take a look at seeking out these birds with a call.

Pheasant

In using the pheasant call, the hunter is calling to locate the bird rather than to actually attract it. Whether to use the strident crow of the cock pheasant or the more subdued "kuk, kuk, kuk, kuk" of the hen will depend upon the length of the hunting season. If the hunting season laps over into the usual breeding period, either of the calls will get results. If the call is that of a hen, the answering cock has the obvious on its mind. A cock that answers another cock is one bent on an argument. The answering bird is sounding off on what it considers to be its territory, and its answer carries warnings against infringement by outsiders. The cock pheasant is a rather ill-tempered bird, always full of fight when intrusion in its territory seems likely. So in this situation good calling can cause a scrappy cock to sometimes approach the call. More likely the case will be that the cock will only reveal its presence and general location by answering the call. It is then up to the hunter to stalk the bird.

Hunter patience and a good ear are the keys to successful pheasant hunting with a call. The call answered most frequently is the simple "kuk, kuk, kuk, kuk" of the hens. This call is made rapidly with decreasing volume, and it is repeated every three or four minutes. Incessant calling without any pauses will only alarm birds that something is phony. The important thing in using this call is to immediately answer the bird back when it responds to your call. Pheasant calling is effective mainly early in the morning and again in the late afternoon. Hens will answer the call of a hen just as readily as does the cock. Here is where a good ear is necessary, for the answering hen will respond in rather subdued tones, not at all like the raucous crow of the colorful cock.

Chukar

The cock pheasant answers a call out of challenge or the bird's interest in sex. The hen pheasant responds in seeking company. Where the chukar partridge is concerned neither challenge nor sex calls are prime movers.

The chukar is a gregarious bird. It loves company and it seeks out company of its kind. When a chukar hears another chukar call, the bird will answer immediately. The exception comes when the bird has just suffered a frightening experience, after which it is prone to remain silent. But where the chukar is concerned, fright wears off pretty quickly. Ten minutes after its fright, the bird is likely to be as talkative as ever.

The most efficient chukar calls are those that are hand operated. There are mouth calls made, but regulating one's breath to get a short, even, fast tempo "kuk, kuk, kuk, kuk" can be a problem. Besides the fast tempo, the call must be sounded almost incessantly, and the amount of blowing necessary can be mighty tiring. The hand-operated call using the bellows principle is far more efficient and easier to use. This call is operated by holding the instrument in the fork between the thumb and first finger. Be sure to keep this hand partially cupped. Then with the fingers of your other hand tap the bellows quickly and firmly. Keep the tapping light because the call of the chukar is neither loud nor harsh.

Like in pheasant calling, the chukar is most receptive to the call early in the morning and late in the afternoon. If the weather is cool and the birds are on the move, chukars will respond quite well even at high noon. The proper way to call this bird is to work slowly and quietly through a field. The only noise you want heard is that of the call, so avoid heavy footfalls, stepping on and snapping twigs, and brushing clothing against bushes. Stop frequently and sound the call. When you get an answer, immediately try to imitate the "call" and stalk toward the spot from which the response came. Don't expect the birds to come to you, although this reaction does occur on occasion.

Quail

The quail is another gregarious bird. It likes company, and it forms into coveys as a measure of mutual safety. Although it is quick to answer a quail call and often when a covey has been broken up it will use the call as a rallying point, there is remarkably little quail hunting done with calls. There are two reasons. First and foremost a good working bird dog is poetry in action. The second reason is that the bob white quail is a master at hiding. If the bird feels secure in its hiding place, it will remain immobile until the hunter literally kicks it out of the brush. If there is not much brush around, this is no real problem. But when the brush is dense, the only sane way to locate the birds is with a good dog sniffing them out. Going from bush to bush yourself is just too time consuming.

The call of the male bob white quail is clear and distinct. An old bob perched atop a fence post can sound off and be heard a quarter-mile away. This in itself is a good reason for using a dog. Even though little actual hunting is done with a quail call, this does not mean good quail hunters view the instrument as a device without merit. I know a lot of bird hunters who employ the instrument at the beginning of the hunt. Rather than turn their dogs loose and have them roam fruitlessly over a field made barren by too much hunting the day before, they work their quail calls seeking out answers from the field. If there are no answers, then they move to another area. The quail call can save a hunter a lot of time and a lot of wear and tear on his dogs.

The quail call is one of the few wildlife calls that has a hole or a series of holes on the top of the instrument. This is necessary in order to produce the proper tones since the same instrument can be used to sound both male and female calls. It is important to be able to produce both calls since there are times when only one sex will answer, and there is no way of knowing in advance which it will be. There are days when only males reply, and there are times when only the hens sound off. And just why I don't know.

The call of the male bob white in effect is simply the words "bob white, bob-bob white." Only to get these sounds you say something else when blowing the call. The "bob white" is easiest to make. Simply blow "to-wit, to to-wit" into the call. Blow lightly to produce the first low note ("to") and then increase air pressure sharply to get the higher note ("wit"). The calls must be sharp and clear. Control your breath to prevent "hissing." Instructions that come with your call will inform which hole or holes to cover—or uncover—to make the call of the hen. There is no point in me trying to instruct which holes to utilize since quail calls of different manufacturers have different placement of holes.

In practical use in the field start with the male call using the two-syllable "to-wit" up to a half dozen times. If birds are in the field and they are prone to answer, the reply will come within a few seconds. When you start getting replies, make a few of your calls the three-syllable "to to-wit." Should you get no response, try the two-syllable sequence again. If you get no replies within a few minutes of calling, you can write the field off. A properly used call can be most helpful in regrouping a covey or helpful in locating a covey that has been scattered.

There are a number of quail calls on the market—all are mouth operated. Some are blown by exhaling; others by "sucking" or inhaling air through the instrument. If you plan to go into quail calling on a serious basis, you should try both types of calls and then purchase the type you find easiest to operate. Personally I prefer the "sucking" or inhale type instrument. I find it easiest to operate, especially so when I am winded after a long hike through the fields. I find I don't get any "hissing" with the inhale type call.

In connection with upland game birds it is interesting to note that calls are being used to determine population trends in given areas. Only in this case it is not man making the calls, but the birds themselves.

Out in Ephrata, Washington, a game biologist for the Washington State Fish and Game Department estimates the number of ringneck pheasants in a given area by counting their caws. He has averaged out that each cock pheasant has four hens in its harem. So he counts the number of cock caws heard in a two-minute period and multiplies by five.

The system he has developed is based on normal pheasant behavior. Barring an unusual disturbance, cock pheasants crow on the average of once every three minutes, give or take a few seconds either way. According to the system, limiting the counting to two minutes eliminates any cock being counted twice. Under good weather conditions the call of the cock pheasant can be heard for approximately a half mile. The Washington state biologist in making his count drives a mile at a time. Then he stops and makes a two-minute count. Then he drives another mile and repeats the procedure. Since territories ruled by cocks normally do not overlap, there is no problem in counting the same bird twice. The system used in the state of Washington is not to determine the exact number of birds in an area, but rather to determine general population trends. The information gathered is used in setting bag limits.

9.

Calling Crows

GOOD PLACES TO HUNT THESE DAYS ARE HARD TO COME BY. YOU either have a good friend to roam the fields with, pay through the nose for a hunting lease, or you join a hunting club.

The tenet in America used to be that wild game belonged to the people. Today it is a tenet in theory only for every day more and more landowners close their property to hunting. This in effect makes *them* the owners of the game, even the migratory species. Even though the landowner must abide by game regulations even when hunting his own property, he still has full control of his land in that he alone determines who can and who can't hunt his land. In short, we have slipped back to the European attitude of the landowner being proprietor of the game.

The hunter himself must shoulder a lot of the blame for what is happening in American hunting. His hunting habits are so lousy—and this is the only way they can be described—that landowners have been forced to nail up "posted" signs to protect their livestock, property, and investments.

Yet there is one kind of hunting that can get a fellow hunting rights on some of this "posted" property. It is black bandit or crow hunting, and it is a type of hunting in which the game call plays a most important role.

This shiny, coal-black winged warrior is a farmer's worst enemy. It strips crops; raids poultry and destroys chicks and eggs; plays havoc with the nests and young of songbirds and many gamebirds. The only nice thing I can say about the black bandit is that it makes a dandy target, and wing shooting them is a fine way to keep your gunning sharp for waterfowl and upland bird shooting. Prove to a farmer that you are willing to spend shells to cull his crow population, and he will give you carte blanche for other kinds of hunting on his property. And if he has a lake or a stream, you can get some fishing rights, too. I have seen crow shooting open lands to sportsmen where money would not buy the time of day.

The crow responds to calling, but it must be good calling. The black marauder is no dolt. It is a highly intelligent bird that can fathom phony calls as easy as a treasury agent can spot counterfeit bills. When the calling is just right, crows will home in in a steady stream. If the hunting is augmented with some strategically placed decoys—a stuffed owl or two will do—a fellow can go through a case of shotgun shells in a day. To emphasize the point, a case of shells is 20 boxes. If you hit with each shell that means 500 birds. That many shots with a shotgun in a single day is a heck of a lot of shooting. Whereas repeated shooting usually drives most game from an area, it does not seem to faze crow flights when good calling and decoys are employed. They just seem to come in an endless stream like Genghis Khan's troops flooding down onto the plains.

The crow is a gregarious bird. It enjoys company of its kind, and the more the merrier. This is most interesting in view of the fact that birds in a flock often get into hellish fights over territorial rights. This aggressiveness makes the bird a willing spectator when the air is filled with sounds of a fight. Crows will respond to calls indicating a fight among crows. Even more attractive is the battle call indicating a crow is having an argument with an owl. These birds take fiendish delight in harassing owls.

And then there is the most enticing call of them all. Crows may be warlike and fight within the clan, but let another black bandit get into trouble and start sounding its distress call and immediately there is a truce. The warring factions put aside their differences and wing to the rescue.

The distress call mixed in with the battle call is a crow-attractor deluxe. When crows are not raising cain destroying crops, nests, and eggs, they are engaged in their favorite pastime of pestering their arch enemy, the owl. An owl atop a limb, being buzzed by a flock of angry crows, reminds one of that epic movie in which King Kong stands atop the Empire State Building and tries to beat off attacking warplanes. How much one shoots in heavy crow population country when the distress call-battle call medley is in full swing depends upon how much punishment a shotgunner's shoulder can take or how much ammunition he has on hand.

Crow hunting is one of the two instances where I personally approve use of the electronic call. The other case is in predator hunting. Actually when one gets down to hardshell cases the crow is as much a predator as the fox and coyote. In some cases the crow may be even more so.

Although calls are made specifically for crows, the bird is one that will respond to several other types of calls. Crows apparently will attack just about anything that can't fight back. I have seen them pecking way at a fatally wounded coyote.

Where crow populations are heavy, the birds will react fairly well to the varmint call, or injured rabbit squeal. In duck nesting country, the crow is the number one destroyer of nests, eggs, and ducklings, and in this respect the duck call can be used to attract the black bandits. The sounds to use are a low feeding chuckle and the nesting duck call. This nesting duck call, which by the way is not worth a hoot in attracting waterfowl, is a low, whispery "kack." Apparently the crows that respond associate these calls with hens likely to be on the nest or have young in tow.

Neither the rabbit squeal nor the duck calls will lure in black bandits by the dozens. These calls are effective only on those lonesome birds flying around in search of an easy meal.

Being in good crow country and using a call and decoys are just part of the ingredients that go into making up a good hunt. As mentioned earlier, this bird is no dummy. It is one of the most intelligent of all wildlife. Crows recognize man as their enemy, and they give man a wide berth. Or let me put it this way, they seem to know exactly how far shotgun pellets will carry, and then they mock man from ten yards outside of that range. That is, they do this as long as they can make out man as a man. So to be successful in hunting these birds man must disguise himself as cleverly as possible. Thus the remaining ingredients for good crow hunting are camouflage clothing and a good hide. The best blinds are those spotted at the edge of the woods. In an open field, haystacks make excellent hides. Crows use flyways in their daily trading back and forth between their roosts and feeding grounds. A blind located in such a flyway coupled with good calling and a few decoys can reward a gunner with some fabulous shooting.

Crow calling and hunting is not as popular as it should be. There are plenty of crows around and there are plenty of places to hunt them. Perhaps the cost of ammunition is causing many hunters to adjust their hunting to taking only choice edible game. Nevertheless crow hunting is a kind of hunting worth pursuing, for it can gain you legal hunting rights on a lot of posted land.

10.

Calling Big Game

BIG GAME HUNTING ON THE NORTH AMERICAN CONTINENT INCLUDES several species of bears, mountain lion, jaguar, moose, elk, caribou, antelope, white-tail deer, mule deer, mountain sheep and goats. Except for deer, moose, and elk, call sounds are of no importance. In fact, sounds and noises are the very things one must avoid. A snapping twig, a falling rock, or a boot scraping against the brush is often just enough to send a bear, sheep, or a goat dashing off to the other side of the mountain.

Cases have been reported of mountain lions and jaguars responding to varmint calls. However, every case I have heard of occurred in Mexico, Central America, or South America where these animals are plentiful. I have not heard of any cases of varmint calls attracting bears. I suppose, however, that if bears were plentiful, this call would get some results.

Moose, elk, white-tail deer, and mule deer do respond to game calls, but their response is inconsistent and in varying degrees. In general the larger the creature the less likely it is to react favorably to game calling. Consequently only a small percentage of big-game hunters use calls. There are really no figures available, and I can only go on estimates. Professional guides estimate that less than ten percent of the hunters seeking moose and elk use calls. Some claim the figure goes up to about 15 percent when deer are involved. Here guides claim most of the deer calling is done by horn rattling. When you get down to varmint hunting, the estimates zoom up to 90 and 95 percent. In waterfowl hunting, duck and goose calls are practically universal. Even if a fellow does not use one, he needs to have one dangling on a cord around his neck in order to look the part of a water-fowl hunter.

In view of the fact that only a small percentage of big-game hunters use calls, the animal species that are susceptible to calling will be treated all in the same chapter.

Moose

The conventional way to hunt moose is to locate the game and then stalk approach to within killing range. Few moose hunters attempt to call their game, although a number of guides do use calls. The call is used to locate the animal as well as to get the creature to expose itself. The moose with its large ears is a real listener. If sounds arouse suspicion, the animal is likely to retreat back into the brush and just watch. Many a tyro hunter has passed within easy range of a moose watching from the brush without ever seeing the animal. It is for this reason that it is advisable for the moose hunter to employ a guide. Let the guide do the calling as well as the watching. Good guides know how to scan the landscape. Most hunters don't have this skill.

Commercial moose horns are available, although most experienced guides make their own out of birch bark. A guide up in Canada's Northwest Territories told me the commercial horns are tops, but he had this to add: "It's better to carry a home-made horn. It's more impressive, and it makes the client feel he has a guide who really knows the works about moose." There is indeed something to be said for appearances making a good impression.

The sound made by the moose call is that of the cow moose. It is most effective during the rutting season. If the bull moose is in the mood, it will make grunting answers, and if the animal has a real urge, it will approach. If the approach is a steady one, then the hunter can be pretty certain the bull is a young one. Older bulls, the ones carrying trophy racks, are extremely suspicious, and they may survey an area for an hour or two before making any kind of approach. The advantage of the call, however, is in getting the creature to expose itself. The bull hidden

from view in the fringes of the brush will often take a step or
two out into the open for better hearing. The alert hunter
knows how to make the most of this little move.

In mountainous country the moose call can be employed to
locate the game. Then the hunter stalks the creature. In lake
country where much hunting is done from canoes, the call is
more effective since these animals more readily expose themselves on lake shores than in wooded, mountainous terrain.

The airplane, especially the light float plane, has done a lot
in pushing the moose call out of the picture. A lot of moose
these days are located by plane. Then the guide sets the plane
down on the lake, and the hunters return by canoe or overland
hike to the area where the animal was spotted.

Elk

The elk is a great wanderer, and locating these fine animals
may take several days in the saddle. As a rule the creatures are
found in high, open timber country and in alpine meadows close
to cover. Consequently long shots are the rule. Some guides feel
the elk horn or bugle is a definite aid in hunting.

Elk travel in herds with a bull maintaining its rule over its
own particular harem but always interested in adding new
mates. The elk bugle is an aid in hunting in that bulls are almost
certain to answer if the call is used during the rutting season.
This in itself can serve the hunter in guiding him in the direction
of a herd. It can be a timesaver since a good elk bugle can be
heard for several miles. After the rutting season neither bulls
nor cows pay much attention to bugling. Bull elks are polyga-
mous, and they collect harems during the September-October
rut. The harem may run from a half dozen to several dozen
cows. The bulls will fight to hold this harem, and if another
mature bull comes into sight, a scrap is sure to follow. Should
the monarch of the harem hear the challenge of another bull,
he will answer in kind and be spoiling for a fight. This challeng-
ing call is a rather high-pitched squeal. Some folks say it sounds
like a whistle. In clear, frosty air this pealing challenge bugle
will carry for a mile or more.

Deer

The most popular big-game call is the deer call, and there are a large number of them on the market. Some work rather well, although in truth a relatively low percentage of deer hunters bother with calls. They would much rather stalk their game, drive it, or simply wait it out from a comfortable blind. Probably the main reason there are so many deer calls is that the deer population in North America is substantially high.

Some of the deer calls work in different ways. All, however, when properly operated produce a low-pitched "blatt" or "bleet," which is supposed to imitate the voice of a doe or fawn. Other calls, which are blown loud and incessantly, produce noises that are supposed to represent a deer in trouble. This particular sound is supposed to appeal to the deer's natural curiosity, and indeed deer are very curious creatures. The really interesting point about it all is that in real life deer seldom make sounds.

In spite of this and in areas where the animals are not hunted hard, the mule deer will come rather well to deer calls. White-tails, on the other hand, are far less receptive. In fact, a lot of deer hunters claim the sounds spook the white-tails rather than attract them. In this respect, some hunters deliberately use the calls on white-tails in order to get them to reveal their presence by moving or stepping out into the open.

A far more productive call for deer is the old-style horn rattling. The clashing of racks coupled with some foot stomping and kicking the surrounding brush seems to appeal to the curious nature of white-tails. The noises made are those of two bucks fighting, and when bucks get to fighting, a doe is certain to be involved. Perhaps the other bucks hearing the scuffle respond just to see if the doe supposedly involved is worth fighting for. The horn rattling trick works, but game regulations vary and in some parts of the country this method of attracting deer is illegal.

While there are a number of deer hunters who use various kinds of deer calls, there is a far greater number of hunters who cuss them. Possibly the bone of contention may revolve around several facts. First and foremost, there is the fact that deer in real life make very few vocal sounds. Perhaps some of the fellows who cuss the calls used theirs too frequently. I know at least a dozen hunters who claim that the only response they got from blown calls was an occasional doe showing herself. If does are legal game, and they are in many areas, this is fine. The hunters I refer to do their gunning in the Texas hill country, which is virtually alive with deer, but like most Texas hunters they disdain in shooting does even though the females may be in season.

I rather suspect these hunters who called and saw does only were not up on their deer-ology. Most deer are not loners. They travel in small groups, a couple to a half dozen or so animals. Bucks almost invariably let does lead the way when they come upon a clearing. It could be a case that these hunters saw the does when they stepped into the open, but their eyes were not trained to pick up the trailing bucks standing just inside the fringe of the thicket.

Calls for waterfowl, crow, varmints, etc., have been proven and are perfected. Perhaps more research is necessary to make the deer call a proven instrument.

11.

Game Isn't Stupid

MANY HUNTERS DO NOT KNOW HOW TO USE THEIR EARS WHEN THEY venture into the wild. They go from one extreme to the other, either hearing nothing or hearing things that are not there. The cause is a combination of ignorance and imagination.

The hunter who hears nothing is the victim of ignorance. The fellow who hears too much is the victim of his own imagination. He is the guy who hears sounds that are not there, and he is the fellow who swings around quickly to get off a fast shot at any brush that moves. He is the character who kills or maims game other than the species he seeks. He is the guy who gives hunting a bad name because the rustle in the bushes sometimes turns out to be another hunter.

These same hunters tend to regard wildlife as being dumb and stupid. Nothing could be more removed from the truth. The animal that is stupid just does not survive in the wild. It has far too many enemies, and it must be ever on the alert if the species is to stave off extinction.

It is interesting to note that the larger the animal the fewer enemies it has. Yet many of our large animals today are on the danger list of becoming extinct because they have so few natural enemies. In the cast of large mammals such as bears, mountain lions, jaguars, and wolves on the North American continent, they have no real enemies other than man. Yet the numbers of these animals are slowly declining because of their inability to live side by side so to speak with man.

Still a large variety of smaller mammals such as deer, foxes, raccoons, rabbits, and squirrels has increased in population. The deer population in the continental United States today is said to be far larger than it was in early Colonial days. This is interesting in view of the fact that the deer has a number of natural enemies other than man. The deer shows remarkable ability to adjust for survival, and this adjustment is a matter of applied intelligence. If deer could speak our language, we probably would be startled to learn that deer see more hunters during the legal hunting season than hunters see deer. If hunters knew how close they came to trophy bucks without seeing them, they would realize that they are matching wits with an intelligent animal. They would also learn that the deer that bounded in and out of sight before they could raise their rifles very likely warned other deer in the vicinity that danger was lurking.

The hunter, whether he seeks to implement his hunting with a game call or not, must know something of the habits and characteristics of the game he seeks. He must also realize that birds and animals communicate and can communicate with their brethren at a considerable distance. Some do it by means of sight, some by sound, others by musk odors they leave behind, and still others by a combination of all the methods listed.

For example, a hen mallard frightened off her pond will sound off series of loud alarm calls that will cause ducks to take wing from other nearby ponds. Or consider the javelina, the little brush pig found in our southwestern states. This little animal, ferocious only in appearance, emits a musk that will warn its kin of danger. It also emits a musk that serves as an assembly point for the herd. The lowly cottontail rabbit will thump the ground loudly with its hind legs to alert other bunnies around that all is not well.

When the hunter learns to recognize the warning signs, sounds, or scents, he can adjust accordingly. Usually the adjustment is little more than sinking down to blend with the terrain and then remaining marble-statue still. Most birds and animals have the distinct characteristic of returning to the area from which they were flushed. The return is thought to be due to curiosity, a trait also found in man. A strange noise or movement on the path will cause a fellow to jump clear. After his initial scare subsides he usually ventures back to learn what caused his fright. Man and wildlife differ in that man returns almost immediately to the scene where the disturbance occurred. Wildlife return to the scene much slower. This return, however, can be hastened with judicious use of a good wildlife call. Perhaps the sight of the hunter moving or the snap of a twig he stepped on caused to game to bolt. Then good game calling comes into play. It can overcome the game's initial fright and arouse its curiosity to investigate. The important thing here is that the hunter must remain absolutely still, for the returning game will be on the alert to react and react swiftly to anything that may seem foreign or out of place.

The game's return will be into the wind for it will depend heavily on scent for something amiss. In this respect the hunter should get well off to one side of the flush area. He will have to watch all areas, and he will have to do so by moving his eyes and not his head. If there is no wind the animal usually makes a complete circle of the area. If there is a wind watch downwind, for the animal's approach will be into the wind. The animal that hunts or approaches its den with the wind is one that moves with part of its defenses down. Animals that do this do not survive long in the wild.

It requires far more time to call in game that has been flushed than it takes to attract the same species from a distance. The game called in from a distance will come in far less suspicious than the recently spooked animal. Remember the spooked animal has within it a war of emotions. One is that of fright and the idea of high-tailing it to the horizon. The other is of curiosity to return to seek out the cause of the disturbance. It will return relatively fast to a vantage point from which it can eyeball the area where the spook occurred. How long it remains in its so-called "spy spot" depends upon the degree of fright it underwent. Again this "spy spot" period can be shortened by good calling. In this case the calling must be unalarming and seductive. It must be a few contented calls and then silence, as continuous calling will allow the game to pinpoint the exact location of the caller. If the animal locates the hunter, it will not bound off in fright. Instead it will slink off stealthily leaving the hunter calling to thin air.

Any time the hunter hears loud, sharp, and rather angry calls a few hundred yards off, and particularly if the calls appear to come from a level higher than himself, he can assume he has been seen. All that game's loud calling does is to alert other species that an enemy is on the prowl. The hunter's only hope in such a case is to quietly vacate the area and move to a new spot a quarter or half-mile away. Then he can resume his calling, and he can be almost certain that he will call in the animal he originally spooked. Except for a few of the larger animals like bears and mountain lions, most species when spooked tend to seek out the company of their kin, for through instinct and training they have learned that it is easier to survive as a member of a flock or herd than it is as a loner.

Even though the various species of wildlife prey upon each other, they have a loose confederation of defense when it comes to man.

The woods and fields are alive with wildlife sounds. This is so when the scene is peaceful and serene. Yet when man intrudes, the area becomes silent. This silence alone is a signal to all wildlife that something is amiss and that possible danger lurks in the vicinity.

In all my years of hunting I have observed this on numerous occasions. To pursue the matter I have made many field trips to observe the reactions of wildlife. The easiest observations were in squirrel territory.

The bushy-tails, of course, fled to safety when I approached their domain. Birds stopped their singing, and the only bird sounds heard were those of whirring wings as the creatures sought out safe perches. I took good hides, being careful to blend in with the native growths and remained absolutely motionless and quiet. Sometimes the waits were long for a renewal of wildlife activity. The first to make their presence known were the birds. They started flittering through the trees, chirping and singing. Then the squirrels made their reappearance. At first it was with utmost caution. Soon they became busy and quite noisy little fellows scurrying around on the forest floor.

In order to reach any valid conclusions it was necessary to make observations with other persons along. A half hour to 45 minutes after I entered the woods my partner would enter and head toward my hide. When my partner came in at a normal walking pace, birdlife became fidgety when the fellow was about five minutes away. The squirrels took the cue, and although

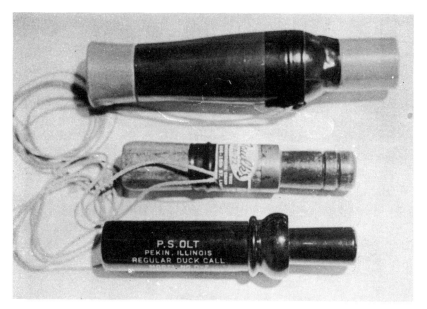

Duck calls come in many sizes and are made of different materials.
Three of the author's are shown above. Top call is made of molded
plastic, center call is of wood, while bottom one is of hard rubber.

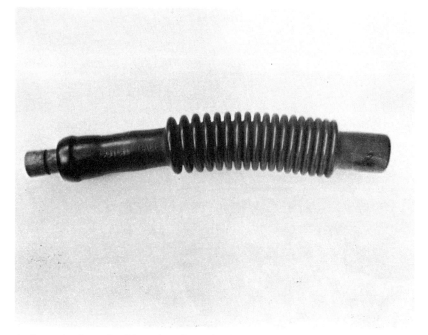

A few duck calls like the Scotch Call are hand operated. When
user shakes this call rapidly, the rubber accordion bellows sounds
duck feeding call.

This shows the inside of a typical duck call. The only moving part is the sounding reed, which vibrates rapidly when air passes over it.

To use duck call properly the instrument should be held in web between thumb and forefinger.

Fingers are then cupped around trumpet end of call to regulate pitch and volume.

Note how call is pressed against lips. If call is taken into mouth, the user's tongue will interfere. User should blow toward ground in order to keep his face from shining through blind.

It takes more than "quacks" to lure ducks. Species like the blue-bill (lesser scaup) respond best to a "brr-r-r-r" sound.

The Hotchkiss Goose Call, like most hand-operated calls in which a piece of slate is used, must be held lightly in finger tips. A "heavy" hold on this call will mute the sound and cut down its range.

To properly operate this squirrel call, user holds sounding trumpet in one hand and taps the rubber bellows with fingers of his other hand.

Sounding box with cedar lid, piece of chalk, and hardwood dowel make up parts of this turkey call.

This call manufactured by the P. S. Olt Co. is a combination owl call and turkey hooter. In crow country, the owl call sounded on this instrument will bring crows to the scene.

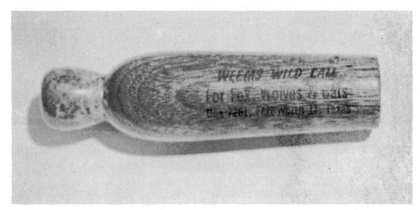

This is a Weems Wild Call, a simple device that is deadly for calling foxes and coyotes.

This quail call is operated best by sucking rather than blowing. It is very effective in locating scattered birds.

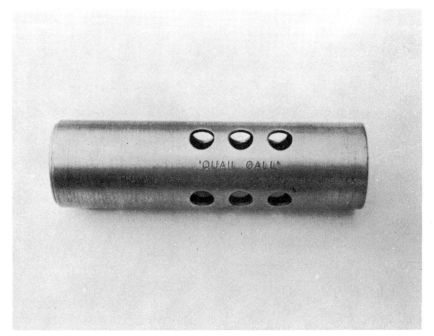

Series of holes on the side of this quail call permit user to sound both male and female calls.

The mourning dove will not respond by coming to calls, but a gentle "cooing" by the hunter can often get nearby birds to reply and reveal their presence.

The crow responds to calling for many reasons, including want of company, curiosity, challenge, and fight.

Don't object to the woodpecker drumming on a nearby tree. The noise of its work seems to assure nearby wildlife that nothing is amiss in the area.

they continued to feed and meander on the ground, they moved appreciably closer to their home base trees. Then when my companion was about 100 yards away, all bird chatter stopped. The squirrels immediately dropped whatever they were doing and most of them scurried part way up their trees. The few bushytails that remained on the ground were quite obviously young and inexperienced fellows. As soon as my partner came into sight, all the squirrels, young and old alike, bolted for cover. Invariably my companions who came in at a steady walk told me they saw little or no game. Their footsteps, the snapping of twigs, and the brushing of their clothing against forest growths had alerted and alarmed all wildlife.

I had other companions make their approach hunter-like. They came into the woods very slowly. They stepped softly and were careful not to step on any twigs or brush that would give off telltale sounds. On a number of occasions I had these fellows well in sight before the birds reacted. In each case they were close enough to the squirrels to bag the animals had they been so inclined. And each time they told me they saw a lot of game as they came through the woods.

This approach to a hunting area is most important. It must be made in such a manner so as not to make every living creature in the woods suspicious. Then when the hunter gets to working his wildlife call, whether it is for squirrels, turkeys, varmints, etc., he is dealing with wildlife that has not been made nervous by the emotion of fright.

12.

Range of Sound

SOUNDS MADE BY SOME LIVING CREATURES CAN BE HEARD FOR MILES. This is to be expected of large mammals such as the moose and elk. The bugling of the bull elk during the rutting season can be heard for miles. One might suppose that the bigger the animal, the louder the sounds it can make. This is not true. Actually the size of the creature has little to do with the range its sounds carry. The cricket is an excellent example. This little rascal is approximately an inch long, yet its chirp hits a note that is audible for almost a mile. Yet the shout of a robust human being, other than an accomplished singer, is extremely difficult to hear a quarter mile away.

Why is it then we can hear some wildlife sounds from great distances yet are unable to project our own voices similar distances?

Audible range depends upon the frequencies of the sound, which is measured in vibrations per second. The normal human ear can detect sounds in a range from 20 to 20,000 vibrations per second. The human voice, however, does not have the range to match. Normal vocal cords can produce sounds in a range from 80 to 853 vibrations per second. It can reach considerably higher and lower in some singers with the range scaling from 42 to 1,408 vibrations per second.

Many species of wildlife, especially animals in the canine and feline families, can hear sounds well above the 20,000 vibrations per second range. Dogs can hear sounds to 30,000 vibrations. Wolves and coyotes are also members of the canine family, and consequently they, too, can hear the sound of the so-called "silent dog whistle," which produces a sound far above man's hearing capabilities. Then why should not these animals respond to the whistle as the dog does?

Just because dogs can hear the "silent dog whistle" does not mean they will react to it. They have to be trained to do so. Wolves and coyotes raised in captivity have been trained to respond to this whistle but only because they were tame enough to train. Blast a feral wolf or coyote with the "silent dog whistle," and the result is a mighty suspicious and nervous animal—an animal too fidgety to lure in close enough for a decent shot.

Man may think he has keen hearing in the ability to discern sounds within the 20 to 20,000 vibrations per second range, but it is nothing when compared with that of a dog. Dogs have such acute hearing that they can hear at 250 yards sounds that most people can not detect beyond 25 yards. A feral dog can hear the same sounds at considerably greater distance than 250 yards. Environment and survival hold the answer.

In order to survive in the wild a creature must depend on its senses, and these senses are keenly developed. I can find no scientific findings to back this up, but I would imagine that the early American Indian had far better hearing than man today. He had to use his hearing to locate both game and enemies. Today we use our ears to absorb the sounds of the industrial complex—super highway system, the tinny crash of pop bands, and the screech of rock and roll singers. And on top of all this we have amplifying systems to magnify these sounds. These noises, which can not be construed as being pleasant, only dull one's hearing range. The environment in which we live is a boon to the hearing aid industry. I feel sure that the domestic dog subjected to this same cacophonous assault is having its hearing ability seriously impaired.

In addition to being able to hear sounds above man's range, animals have the added advantage of being able to move and turn their ears to pick up sounds from different directions. A wild animal's ears are remarkably like the radar antenna that revolves atop an airport terminal. The only difference is the radar antenna revolves 360 degrees, while the ears of animals move rhythmically back and forth in a semi-circle. When a particularly interesting or foreign sound is picked up, the animal's ears stand erect to form a receiving cone to better fathom the noise.

How fast and how far a sound travels depends upon the density of the conductive agent. At 32 degrees F. sound travels through air at a speed of 1,100 feet per second. In water the speed is 5,700 feet per second since water is approximately five times denser than air. If the conductor is brick or concrete, the speed is upped to 11,900 feet per second, and if the conductor is steel, sound speed is increased to 16,400 feet per second. The speed with which sound travels determines to a certain degree how far it can be heard. Since we are concerned with sounds and calls that attract animals and birds, we need only take into consideration sound speed in air. The speed increases approximately by a foot for each one degree increase in temperature. If the calling is being done in 90 degree temperature, the speed of sound is 1,168 feet per second. Although in terms of time this is only a fractional part of a second faster, it does mean the sound will be picked up a little more distinctly by the game. It also means the sound will carry just a little further. Actually the increase is so small that it is negligible.

The spot from which the hunter sounds his call has a lot to do with how far the sound carries. The call sounded from the top of a hill has greater reach than the same call made from the lowest part of the valley. One must always keep in mind that matter has acoustical properties. Some forms of matter absorb or cushion sound; others reflect it. The sound that may carry a mile across an open field will have far less range in the deep forest. If the caller gets the bright idea to greatly increase volume when calling in the deep woods, he is almost certain to defeat his purpose. Except in the case of electronic calls on which volume controls are available, both blown and hand-operated calls are designed to work under average pressure. Blowing too hard into the mouth call will result in the familiar "pig squeal," and this is not at all effective unless the game sought is a large predator. When too much pressure is applied on the hand-operated call, the resulting sound will be either a screech like a piece of chalk on a blackboard or a dull-sounding wooden grate. Both are out of character for wildlife, and any game response will be one of curiosity, which is a rather weak mood. Curiosity is a mood that is likely to be aroused just before suspicion. And right after suspicion comes the mood of fright, the one feeling you do not want to arouse in any game.

The answer to using the game call successfully in the deep woods should be rather obvious. Instead of trying to cover a huge area by volume alone, the hunter must cover the woods by moving from spot to spot. This, too, can be overdone. Moves every five minutes are of no use. The proper way is to take a stand and wait about five minutes before doing any calling. This period of silence is important in that it allows wildlife in the immediate area to overcome its initial fright and settle back down to the routine of normal life. Then start sounding the call. If you get no response in 15 or 20 minutes, move to a new stand at least a quarter mile away and repeat the procedure all over again. A good average would be to make two moves every hour. In four hours of hunting, the total of eight moves will allow you to cover a lot of territory. This procedure will stand up very well for turkey, predator, coon, squirrel, and deer calling. If only predators are sought, then three moves per hour work out fine. These beasts tend to respond on the trot, sometimes even on the run.

13

What Made That Sound?

ONE HAS TO ASK QUESTIONS TO GET ANSWERS, FOR QUESTIONS ARE the avenues to education. The best outfitted hunter in the land only stamps himself as a tyro when he repeatedly asks: "What made that noise?" If he was half the hunter his wearing apparel would suggest him to be, he would be able to recognize the source of most sounds encountered afield. Sound recognition is of the utmost importance if he plans to augment his hunting with a game call. He must also know when game will likely make sounds and when it will remain silent.

For example, even in the finest quail country the bobs won't answer a call if they sense a predator roaming in the vicinity. I experienced an interesting case on a quail hunt. My hunting companion and host used a quail whistle to learn the general location of coveys in the field before he loosed his dog. On this particular morning he got not a single "peep" answer to his whistle, although he knew the field contained at least a half dozen coveys. He was far better at listening than I was, for all of a sudden he pocketed the quail whistle and fished out a varmint call. In less than ten minutes of squealing he lined the front bead up on a fox and clobbered it with a load of 12-gauge No. 4 shot. Then he explained to me that while he was using the quail whistle, he had picked up a whine and several low rasping barks. He immediately identified the source as a roaming fox and put the varmint call to work. I had missed the fox sounds because subconsciously I had shut my ears to all sounds except those of quail.

Wildlife's ability to sense danger is uncanny. After smoking a cigarette over the remains of the fox, my friend put his quail whistle back to work and got almost immediate response from two different parts of the field. Then he explained to me what he knew I thought was a strange way of hunting quail. It was simply that his dog had a wandering mind and was not above chasing a fox or bobcat if it picked up fresh scent. Most bird dogs—if they have been trained properly—disdain to truck with anything other than quail.

Waterfowl are garrulous. They are talking all the time. The only time they are silent is when they are sleeping. Just about everyone is familiar with the sounds waterfowl make. The same holds with crows and quail, for their calls are distinct and loud.

There are other species of wildlife, however, that are relatively quiet. Often the sounds they do make can not be heard at any distance. Consequently a lot of hunters, even those skilled in the use of wildlife calls, are unfamiliar with the normal every-day sounds many animals make. Learn to recognize sounds and you will get far more enjoyment out of your game calling. There will be times when the game you call never shows itself, yet you know of its presence by the sounds it makes.

Let's take up the communication sounds of various animals. We'll start with the little fellow, the squirrel, and work up to the big one, the moose.

GRAY SQUIRREL—The most common sound this rodent makes is a sharp "bark." The animal can vary the tones of its "bark" to denote anger, fear, or defiance. When extremely angry, the gray squirrel will chatter its teeth. It also makes a purring sound, which at times can sound like a buzz.

FOX SQUIRREL—It "barks" like the gray squirrel, but a sound it makes far more frequently is similar to the "cluck" we make with our tongues. The animals chatter their teeth when angry. The fox squirrel's repertoire is complete with grunts, slight coughs, and churring sounds.

RACCOONS—These animals make a wide variety of sounds ranging from a contented churring coming from far down in the chest to actual screams. The churring is much like that of the house cat, only greatly amplified. When angry an adult raccoon will growl, hiss, or give a rasping bark. If the animal gets into a fight, the growl, hiss, and bark are liberally spiced with a lot of screams.

GRAY FOX—This animal is capable of hissing, whining, growling, yapping, barking, and squalling. Its rasping bark is heard mainly during the breeding season and in the summer when parent animals are teaching the pups to hunt.

RED FOX—It makes the same sounds as the gray fox, only its bark is higher pitched. Females frequently squall, while the males are more prone to barking.

BOBCAT—Cats, wild or domestic, can meow, hiss, growl, squall, spit, and scream. When contented, all cats purr. These are the sounds of the feral bobcat. They differ from those of the common house cat only in that they are much louder. In the case of large bobcats, their entire bodies appear to quiver when they are purring. During the mating season they can turn the dark into a nightmare with their love laments. When you hear low yowls that grow in intensity, you can pretty well bet a pair of bobs are in the very act of mating. And then when they scream, they tear the night apart. The important thing to remember about the bobcat is that when the animal is hunting, it remains totally silent.

COYOTE—This animal has a yapping, barking howl, and almost anything can cause a coyote to go into its long, incessant howl. The animal also growls, whines, and squalls. It makes distinct barks when extremely suspicious.

WOLF—Whether the wolf is gray or red, it whines, cries, and growls but very rarely barks. Those that do any amount of barking are usually juveniles. The long drawn-out howl is the most familiar sound made by the wolf, and it is a real spine-tingler. Once you hear it you will never forget it. Wolves, however, are relatively scarce today, and few city-bred hunters are ever likely to hear the howl.

WHITETAIL DEER—This animal has quite a repertoire of sounds, but they are seldom heard except by the most attentive of hunters. Probably the reason is the sounds they make don't have much range and some of them are quite like the sounds made by domestic sheep. Young fawn bleat like a lamb, while adult deer sound not unlike hoarse, raspy sheep. Adults can also whistle and snort through their noses. The whitetail makes one sound that has good range, but unless a hunter knows what to listen for, he will miss it completely. The sound is that of stamping feet. The vibrations can be felt a considerable distance and apparently they serve as a means of alerting other deer of possible danger.

MULE DEER—This deer makes sounds similar to those of the whitetail. Mule bucks also make a coughing grunt.

ELK—The elk is famous for its high-pitched bugling. It is a scream, warning, and challenge all rolled into one. It is sounded frequently during the breeding season when the bucks are out on the search, but after rutting is over, the bulls rarely make any sounds for the remainder of the year. Cow elks occasionally bugle, but their sounds are much softer and of less range than those of the bulls. Cows also squeal and cough, although neither sound has any appreciable range. Elk calves bleat and sound almost calflike.

MOOSE—The most common sound is a deep grunting cough made by both bulls and cows. That of the bull is deep and raspy. The calves have a high-pitched bleat. In anger and during the rutting season bulls also snort and bellow. Most all of the sounds made by moose are quite like those of the domestic cow. The basic difference is the lack of contentment found in the sounds of domestic cattle. The call of the moose has a lot of challenge in it.

Game calls are of little help when it comes to hunting such American big game like pronghorn antelope, bighorn sheep, Dall sheep, and mountain goat. Nevertheless it behooves the hunter to be able to recognize the sounds made by these animals.

PRONGHORN ANTELOPE—The adult doe makes a low-pitched blat sound. When angered or surprised both sexes snort loudly. Young pronghorn kids make a high-pitched quivering bleat that carries a considerable distance.

BIGHORN SHEEP—Rams occasionally make a raspy blat, while ewes have a guttural blat. The lambs bleat. All the sounds are much like those of domestic sheep.

DALL SHEEP—This species sounds are quite similar to those of the bighorn sheep.

MOUNTAIN GOAT—In addition to soft grunting, this animal makes sounds similar to those of domestic sheep.

Even if a hunter does not employ a wildlife call, he should for his own safety be able to recognize the source of most sounds he hears in the field. Perhaps I should broaden the statement to include anyone—hunter, fisherman, bird or game watcher—who ventures into the wild.

Perhaps a few personal experiences will serve to illustrate the point.

One involved a fishing trip on an oxbow lake just off the Sabine River, the boundary line between Texas and Louisiana. We were fishing the marshy end of the lake from an aluminum johnboat. One little neck looked particularly inviting. We had barely paddled into the mouth when I heard a hissing sound. The first thing that comes to mind when one hears hissing in the wild is that there is a snake nearby. I recognized the hiss immediately as belonging to a critter considerably larger than a snake. I back-paddled swiftly and moved the boat out to open water. It was then that the source of the hiss showed itself, and it did so with a considerable bellow thrown in for good measure. It was an adult alligator. It only showed its head from alongside a muskrat mound, but I guessed it to be a six or seven footer.

It had challenge in its eyes and bellow—and for good reason. Two small baby gators about a half-foot long each were struggling to get out of the water and under their mother's protective wing. Before we had attempted to paddle into the neck I had seen one of the baby gators swimming near the bank. I knew what situation we could possibly face, but I did not expect protective mom gator to be around so close. At least I had not seen her when I eyeballed the bank, and I thought I had done a pretty good job of eyeballing, too. Then when I heard the hiss I knew the mother alligator was close. It was a sound I had encountered on several occasions when I confronted gators on marsh duck hunts. Only in the case of the duck hunts, the gators had no young around, and they beat a quick retreat. This gator, however, had young and she was dead set on protecting her ground.

I don't want this to sound as though alligators are bellicose monsters that seek out to destroy man. Actually they are shy and retiring, and they will beat a hasty retreat. The exception comes when they have young, and then their maternal and protective instinct comes to the fore. I don't think this particular gator would have actually attacked our boat, unless we had approached straight in on it. As it was we would have passed it by a good 40 feet. It might have been different with a couple of fellows unaccustomed to coming so close to a feral gator. Again I don't think the gator would have attacked them, but the sudden fright might have been enough for them to upset their boat. The story they would bring home then would be certain to be the one about "the gator that tried to attack us." I fear of lot of wild creatures have far wilder reputations than they deserve simply because of the stories related by inexperienced outdoorsmen.

Another experience was quite funny. A youngster in our party went into the woods early one morning to hunt squirrels. About a half hour later he came back running and breathless. He rushed into the kitchen of the farm house, and to hear him tell it there was "a heck of a big snake just a hissing and a hissing inside a hollow log." No, he did not look into the log. He just heard the hiss when he stepped over it. Every time he stepped, he heard another hiss. So he decided a rapid retreat was in order. He told the farmer where the log was located, and the fellow allowed he would stroll down for a look after he finished his coffee. Finally he picked up his .22 rifle, grabbed a tow sack off the back porch, and headed for the woods. At the insistence of the youngster, we all trooped along.

Sure enough when he neared the log we heard the hissing. The farmer got down on all fours, sighted down his .22, and fired. Hissing, squalling, screaming resulted. Dead bark and dust flew off the log as if it had come alive. The farmer fired three or four more .22 rounds and then all was quiet. Then he kicked away a pile of leaves and twigs at the mouth of the log, picked up a piece of chain, and started pulling. Out came a trap with a bullet-riddled and very dead four-legged, furry, bob-tailed "snake." And the farmer was quite happy in the fact that there was one less bobcat around to make nocturnal raids on his poultry.

I doubt if an experienced woodsman would have recognized the initial hiss the boy heard as that of a bobcat. But the point is he would not have panicked. He would have probed to find the true identity. Quite likely he would have struck the log with a length of dead limb, and I'm sure the bobcat would have replied with a squall instead of a hiss.

An interesting sidelight on wildlife is that most species of animals and birds can and do hiss. I have invariably encountered this hissing in trapped or severely wounded game and often in meeting up with females either with young or when guarding their nests or dens. It apparently is a challenge, a show of defiance. It leads me to rather suspect that a good many folks who heard a "snake hissing under the brush" actually heard the sound made by a gravely wounded and dying animal or bird. Had they been females with young, nest, or den, the creatures probably would also have revealed themselves. They come into the open to either drive off the intruder or to lead the invader away from the area. At least this has been my experience along this line.

14.

Ear for Sound

IT IS IMPOSSIBLE TO WRITE A BOOK OR AN ARTICLE, EVEN FICTION, without having to do considerable research. A lot of research went into the preparation of this book, but in so doing I ran into an aspect I had not anticipated. I undertook this book project feeling that I could offer the average sportsman a wealth of information. Then after purely by chance hitting upon a certain part of the research, I changed my view from "feeling I could offer" to a more positive "knowing I could offer."

It started in a waterfowl calling chat with a group of duck hunters waiting for the hunting camp manager to assign blinds. One word led to another and soon I had my duck call out to make various calls to illustrate my views.

One fellow in the group remarked: "Man, that really sounds good. Just like an old greenhead mallard."

His compliment pleased me, and, of course, I started to add a little more finesse to my calling. This in turn caused him to comment again.

"I can just see that old greenhead up there answering back. Quacking exactly like you're doing. I just love to hear those old greenheads quack."

Right there it hit me. This guy was either no duck hunter or he had the worst ears in the world. I stopped blowing the call and answered: "This is a mallard call, but the call isn't that of a greenhead. This is of a hen mallard. The greenhead drake makes an altogether different sound."

Before the fellow had a chance to either voice his ignorance or bust me in the mouth, the hunting camp manager stepped in and said: "That's right. Drakes and hens don't sound alike."

In the next several weeks and without telling hunters why, I buttonholed 200 hunters, not all in a group but in singles and pairs. I asked questions about the sounds that hens and drakes make. I was astounded to discover that 141 did not know there was a difference. They simply assumed that all ducks, regardless of sex or even species, sounded alike. Even more astounding was the fact that each of the 200 fellows interviewed professed to regularly using duck calls.

I went down into the marshes with some of these fellows, too, and encountered some almost unbelievable incidents. I've had fellows mistake the croaking of a frog for the quacking of a duck. It was shocking to learn that folks with ears did not know how to use them.

This duck sound investigation led to other avenues. Out of 100 fellows who hunted rabbits, an even 70 said they had never heard a crippled rabbit scream. Some said they had heard wounded bunnies loudly thump the ground with their hind legs. Percentages were a little better with the 100 squirrel hunters questioned. Seventy-eight said they had heard and could identify squirrel "barks." Twenty-one of 30 fellows who hunted coyotes thought the animals only howled. They did not know that coyotes can bark too.

All the pieces began to fall into place, and it became obvious that where the average hunter is involved, well over half can't recognize the sounds of the game they seek. It is not a case of being stupid. It is a case of a serious lack of experience. Why?

Urbanization holds the answer. It has put perhaps 90 percent of the hunters out of contact with wildlife. You can't go hunting a half dozen times a year and be expected to identify the source and cause of the wildlife sounds around you unless you know what to listen for in the first place.

I enjoy hunting and fishing. I do not like to partake of either sport alone. I enjoy company. And I enjoy hunting with tyros as much as I do with experts. Some folks I know hunt with tyros just so they can impress the beginners with their skill. I enjoy tyro hunting companions, too, but for a different reason. Their mistakes serve to jog my memory bank on things not to do. In fact, learning from a beginner's error is often easier than learning from an expert's finesse.

Cows "moo," horses "whinny," and pigs "oink." After that, far too many hunters are lost when it comes to game sounds. And the more the concrete and asphalt cancers spread, the less wildlife area there will be in which to enjoy the sounds of nature. With the world's population increasing by geometric leaps and bounds, there may come the day when wildlife greenery and its inhabitants become solely museum pieces. Then, of course, there will be no need for wildlife calls or for hunting or for fishing. Our whole lives then will probably revolve around pills.

From Colonial times until the industrial zoom created by World War II, the bulk of the American population resided in rural or semi-rural areas. It used to be a kid's upbringing was not complete until he owned a single shot .22 rifle. The country boys could practically hunt off the homestead back porch. The kids in the hamlets and villages could reach fair to middling hunting inside the space of a ten-minute walk. Even those youngsters raised in small cities were quite close to good wild-life terrain. This, of course, was in the days when wildlife habitat abruptly started where the city limits stopped. The suburban craze had not yet begun.

There was no television to watch, the surfboard was still ex-clusively property of Hawaii, and the turned-on generation had not yet been visioned. Consequently, .22 hunting was a way of life for a vast number of kids in their early teens. They spent many hours in the fields and woods. Their ears, not yet assaulted by the din of rock and roll, were in tune with the times. They listened when they hunted. They learned the various sounds made by a wide variety of wildlife, and they learned to imitate these sounds. They made all their calls with their vocal cords, for in those days the only known commercial calls were those for ducks and geese.

We learned the various whistles of birds, and we used these calls. We did not use the calls in the light of seeking to bring the birds to us, but rather to get them to expose themselves enough for a clean shot. What held true with bird life also held for small game. We all hunted with open iron sights. Scopes were unheard of as far as most kids were concerned. Those of us who had heard about scopes viewed them as exclusive prop-erty of the rich.

We learned wildlife calls and wildlife habits by association and frequent exposure. The big fault of the times then was a lack of conservation knowledge. We may have gone hunting primarily for squirrels, but if a woodpecker, blue jay, robin, etc., presented itself as a tempting target, we fired away. We never went home until we fired all the shells in our pockets. Through ignorance we destroyed a lot of game that should have been passed. Nevertheless we learned far more about wildlife than the average youth of today will ever learn in a lifetime.

Today the bulk of the American population is urbanized. Even the fellow who lives in a small city may have to drive an hour at high speed to reach country inhabited by legal game. The poor Joe in the metropolitan complex may have to spend half a day fighting urban and then highway traffic to reach decent hunting grounds. In fact, if most fellows kept a log on each hunting trip, they would be shocked to learn that approximately half of the time of each hunt is spent in traveling to and from the area hunted. Consequently, this fellow must squeeze the utmost out of every hour in the field in order to harvest game. He does not have the time to just loll around and listen to the sounds of the fields and forests.

Many wildlife sounds can be duplicated by the human voice. Hunters of decades ago had this skill, but they had it because they came in frequent contact with wildlife. Today's average hunter does not have this advantage of frequent association. He could master the art with his own voice—if he had the time to listen. But he does not have this time, so he has to take the next best course and use commercial calls. These calls, whether blown or hand operated, will produce the correct sounds with a minimum of effort. All the modern user need do is practice to get the correct sequence, tempo, and volume. Then all he needs is confidence in the instrument.

I know some musicians who are real artists with wildlife calls. They have the ear for sounds, and after hearing a call a couple of times they can get it down pat. In fact, I know one musician-hunter, a fellow with a real pioneer spirit, who has called foxes and coyotes with his clarinet. He can really turn out lifelike rabbit-in-agony sounds. He did it in the interest of experimenting. He does not use the clarinet for hunting, for it is far too expensive an item to take out in the wind, rain, sand, and what-not.

Since World War II days wildlife calling has come into its own. The many manufacturers have perfected calls with printed or recorded instructions for a wide variety of animals and birds. Their public relations people have done a good job in selling the American hunting public a bill of goods. And I might add it is a mighty "sound" bill of goods.

Game calling is no fly-by-night venture or passing fancy. It is an established art that is here to stay. There are today a number of companies that manufacture a great variety of calls. All started little and have grown into thriving business.

For example, consider the P. S. Olt Company that was founded by Philip S. Olt in 1904. He invented a call that worked so well his friends around Pekin, Illinois, urged him to obtain a patent on it. In the first year of business, his company sold 600 calls. By our present-day standards an annual sale of 600 units is not enough to pay material costs, but remember this was back in 1904. It was before mass advertising and the 40-hour work week and at a time when all game was plentiful.

From sales of 600 in the first year, the P. S. Olt Company has prospered and today it is the world's largest manufacturer of game and bird calls. Operated now by Arthur E. Olt and James R. Olt, the company makes 31 different calls, one for nearly every type of hunting. Olt calls today are worldwide in distribution.

It stands to reason that wildlife calling should be more popular here in America than elsewhere in the world. Where else in the world do citizens have such free access to sporting arms? And where else in the world does the average man have so much money and spare time? At this writing we here in the United States enjoy a 40-hour work week. There are some labor leaders —and they have no small number of politicians on their side— who are advocating work weeks of 35 to 32 hours. Look at it this way: The seven-day week has 168 hours; 40 goes for work; another 56 hours is consumed by sleep; that leaves 72 hours in which to get into trouble—or to spend in some fruitful vocation like hunting or fishing.

The use of wildlife calls is being spread to other countries, but it is being spread by the Americans who make the foreign hunting jaunts. So many Americans are making these trips that the art of game calling is bound to catch on. Several acquaintances who have made African and Indian hunting safaris tell me that they have had gunbearers and trackers who made voice sounds to catch the attention of various game species.

I have heard some second-hand stories of African lions being called in on the run. The story-tellers never told me what kinds of calls were used. I would assume, however, that the varmint call that works so well on our fox, bobcat, coyote, and wolf would do equally as well with lions. Predators have one trait in common—that is to prey upon animals in distress.

15.

Reactions to Sound

ALL WILDLIFE—ANIMALS, BIRDS, AND FISH—REACT TO SOUND. IF THE sound is sharp and foreign to the creature's environment, the reaction is one of fright and flight from the immediate scene. The crack of a rifle shot will cause nearby wildlife to scurry for cover. More distant wildlife may not bolt, but the reaction of the creatures will be one of increased wariness and suspicion. The sound of men's voices can be just as startling, although the range of one's voice will be only a fraction of that of the gun shot.

Good fishermen, those who score consistently on trip after trip, are fellows consciously aware of sound. They refrain from unnecessary talking. If they are wading, they move slowly and carefully so as not to cause any needless fuss in the water. The fellow who wades rapidly causes a commotion much like that of large predators trying to catch fish in shallow water. Many a fisherman has waded into the water like a charging fullback and has been rewarded with the sight of a lot of Vs across the surface. The Vs are always caused by frightened fish vacating the area. Boat fishermen exercise extreme care to avoid bumping the sides and bottom with paddles, tackle, or their feet. The resulting sound causes a jolt that fish many feet away can feel. This aspect of noise is something the "I never catch anything" Joes fail to take into consideration. What may sound like a minor noise to them is major as far as fish are concerned. They fail to realize—or perhaps don't know—that water is five times as dense as air and is an excellent conductor of sound. The "little bump" that can be heard 20 feet away in the air can be felt by fish under water 100 feet away.

Early in 1970 the Texas Parks and Wildlife Department conducted some observations with various species of salt-water fish. The main observation was to see how the fish reacted to tags imbedded in their bodies, and, of course, the work had to be done with captive fish placed in an impoundment. One of the most interesting observations noted had to do with sound. Fishermen who seek the channel bass—a fish known as the redfish in Gulf of Mexico waters—use extreme caution when wade-fishing in shallow water. The thump of footsteps can cause these fish to scoot for the protection of deep water. Channel bass put in the impoundment also scooted when they felt the footsteps of the marine biologists walking the banks. Yet a curious thing evolved with these captive fish. They were fed by the workers and they soon learned to associate the fall of footsteps on the bank with chow time. And they reacted accordingly. The findings in this case certainly prove that fish have the capacity to learn. It should also prove another point. Don't go to the zoo and expect to learn animal behavior. After an animal, bird, or fish overcomes its fear of man and comes in daily contact with him, the creature's reactions to humans are different from those in the feral. The wild game caller, whether he is hunter or just watcher, must know feral behavior for he certainly will not be dealing with tame or semi-tame game in the woods and fields.

The outdoorsman can use the finest game calls and still not attract game if he inadvertently or carelessly injects foreign sounds between calls. The outdoorsman who sounds his call and then insists on carrying on conversation with his buddy is seriously penalizing himself and his companion. Save the idle chatter and gossip for the elbow-bending session back at the camp.

Sounds that attract game play on one or all of several moods —curiosity, company, hunger, anger, or sex. With some species of wildlife, all five come into play. The basic reason most game responds to a call is hunger. With a few species, especially the varmints, an "easy meal" is most likely the only reason they respond to a call. In this connection note that the call most attractive to foxes, wolves, coyotes, etc., is one that imitates a wounded rabbit. This distress call signifies to the predator that an easy meal is up for grabs. This wounded rabbit squeal, by the way, will not attract other rabbits.

Waterfowl react to calls basically for company and food. Fish reaction to sound is basically out of curiosity and for food. With fish, however, there is a third reason, which in the case of some species is very pronounced. It is best described as a sound that arouses anger within the fish, and it is most effective when fish are nesting. Obviously it is a case of a fish protecting its territorial domain.

The basics of all game calls are (1) to imitate the sounds of the wildlife species sought, and (2) to imitate the sounds of something upon which the sought wildlife feeds. In principle these calls are for the purpose of bringing the game to the hunter. To a lesser degree there are a few calls made for the purpose of the hunter locating his game. When these calls are used, the reaction of the game sought is to answer vocally. The quail, elk, and moose calls are good examples. These calls can clue a fellow in as to whether or not an area contains the game species he desires.

Earlier in this chapter I mentioned that sudden, foreign noises cause game to flee from an area. Some unusual sounds, however, can stop moving game. These out of character sounds won't stop it for long, but the halt is usually long enough for the hunter to get off a well-aimed shot. These strange sounds will not work with game that is already half-frightened out of its wits. They will only make the game move that much faster. It is a different story, however, with the unsuspicious game that is following its normal every-day movement pattern.

A deer trotting across a clearing can often be brought to a complete halt by a shrill blast on a whistle. The animal will stop and look toward the source of the sound. The pause will not be long—not more than five or six seconds—but it will be enough time for the hunter to scope the animal and get off his shot. This same shrill whistle will bring a bounding rabbit to a skidding stop. You can frequently get the same reaction with an auto horn.

The unusual, foreign sound can be an attraction for at least two species of waterfowl—the redhead duck and bluebill (scaup). In the case of each species, the sound is solely for the purpose of attracting attention. It will not bring the fowl to the hunter. The only way these foreign noises play any part at all in luring in the birds is when the hunter is shooting over a decoy rig. The noise catches the attention of the birds, and when they turn their heads to pinpoint it, they see the decoys. Bluebills and redheads have one thing in common: they love to join company on the water, and in they zip.

I hunted with a guide several times on Copano Bay near Corpus Christi, Texas, a part of the Gulf that is alive with pintails and redhead ducks. The guide used to beat on the bottom of a five-gallon metal drum to catch the attention of the redheads. The birds did not come to the decoys every time, but it happened often enough for one to realize the drum beating did catch their attention. I have seen the same thing accomplished many times with a shrill whistle. This is not calling game by any stretch of the imagination. It is simply catching their attention. If the birds are not frightened and you have a good show of decoys on the water, chances are good they will decide to join company.

In the hands of the expert, the wildlife call can be as deadly as the actual bullet that puts game in the bag. The same call used by the tyro can be an instrument of game conservation. No wildlife call, whether mouth or hand operated or battery powered, is worth the material it is made of if the user employs it incorrectly. Sounding the call so it mimics the noises attractive to the game sought is just the start of the picture. In order to complete it and make it a first-rate show, the user must know where, when, and how often to use it. For example, the duck hunter who starts "kack, kack, kacking" on his call the minute he deposits himself in the blind and continues to call incessantly until the minute he heads for home is going to attract darned few birds. In fact, even though his "kacks" may sound like the real thing, too much calling will permit the birds to pinpoint the source of the sound. They see unnatural movement in the rushes, a shiny face or light reflecting off a fellow's glasses, and they hightail it out of range. In short, too much calling can be worse than no calling at all.

In this connection, any fellow bent on augmenting his hunting by using a call should learn the habits and characteristics of the game he seeks, implicitly follow the instructions that come with the call, buy a record demonstrating use of the call, spend long hours practicing the art, and finally—this is most important— think like the bird or animal he seeks.

16.

The Right Mood

IN ORDER TO BE SUCCESSFUL WITH THE WILDLIFE CALL, THE USER must know what mood or moods he needs to stimulate in the game sought. With some species only one mood will move them. With others several different moods will cause them to respond, yet at various times of the year only one can be stimulated consistently. A good example is the wild turkey. In areas where spring hunting is allowed, the mating call is a sure-fire game-getter. This same mating call is next to useless in the fall because the toms, young and old alike, have had their fill and could care less. But in the fall the "lost bird" and "assembly" calls that are ineffective in the spring will produce results. In short, if you are to enjoy success with the wildlife call, you must fit the call to the prevailing mood of the year. The user might keep in mind that old dodge about variety being the spice of life.

Number one in wildlife calling, whether it is for animals or birds, is to know the habits and characteristics of the game. Is it gregarious or is it a loner? Does it work to open areas or is it a woods creature? Does it vocally answer the call or does it approach silently? Is it active during the day or are its habits strictly nocturnal? If the outdoorsman does not know the answers to these questions, he is in the same boat with the fellow who goes to the football game and does not get a program.

Let's consider a few examples. Generally speaking the fox is a loner. It may work with its mate or young tagging along, but families do not clan up to form packs. So no matter how well you can imitate the barks and yaps of a fox, you are going to enjoy little success in getting other foxes to respond. These animals respond to fox sounds only during the mating season.

This alligator really isn't as close as it seems. Its photo was taken through telephoto lens by the author. The gator left the bank and started swimming in when the author sounded a series of grunts. Gators today are on the protected list in all states.

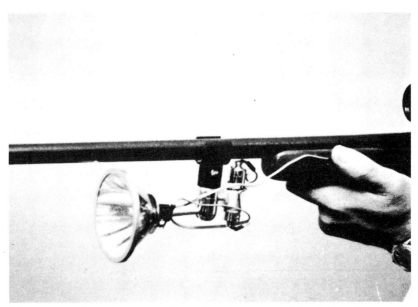

Varmint calling is especially effective at night. A hunter must have some kind of light attached to his gun for effective shooting. (Courtesy A-1 Manufacturing, Inc.)

The right game calls and gun light rewarded these night hunters with a fox, two coons, and a ring-tailed cat. (Courtesy A-1 Manufacturing, Inc.)

This hunter with his bag of game is well equipped for both day and night hunting. His camouflage suit is perfect for day hunting. For night shooting, he has hunting lights mounted on hat as well as on rifle. Note his hunting was augmented with electronic call. (Courtesy A-1 Manufacturing, Inc.)

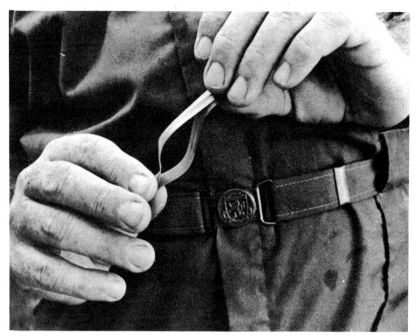

Two blades of grass can be fashioned into an on-the-spot varmint call.

Grass blades are stretched tight. Wounded rabbit squeal is produced by blowing sharply on edge of the blades.

Two half-dollar pieces can be used to produce squirrel bark. One coin must be held in palm of hand with care taken so only edges of coin contact flesh.

Second coin is held with thumb and forefinger of other hand and then struck edgewise against center of coin in other hand. Striking should be done sharply to produce "barking" sound.

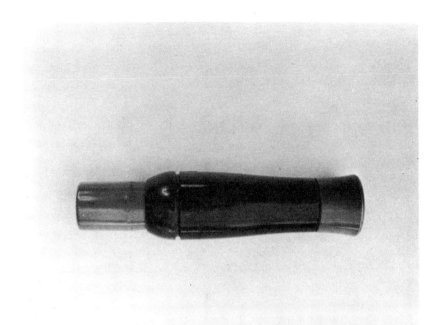

Top photo shows assembled duck call. Lower photo shows same call stripped into component parts. The small white pebble-like objects fit in special section of mouthpiece to absorb moisture. All parts must be dry for call to operate properly.

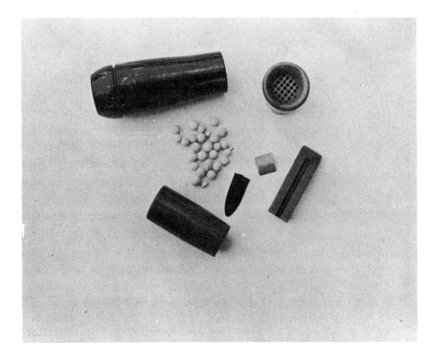

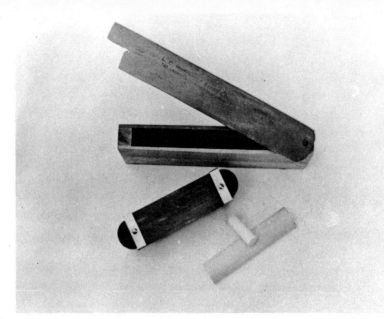

Extra care must be exercised when using hand-operated box calls such as this goose call (top) and turkey call (bottom). Neither call will operate properly if wet. Care must also be taken so as not to split the cedar lids.

This is an assortment of noise-making or fish-calling lures. The plugs with inverted wing-like lips (top left, top right) produce a "gurgle, gurgle, gurgle" sound on steady retrieve. Top center and bottom left plugs have faces that make a "pop" when rod is jerked. The other two lures make a "chug" sound when rod is worked.

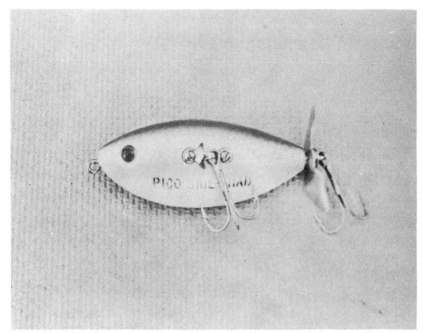

Propeller on this Pico Side Shad revolves rapidly on retrieve and makes a fluttering "plip-plip-plip" sound remarkably similar to the noise made by a crippled minnow struggling on the surface of the water.

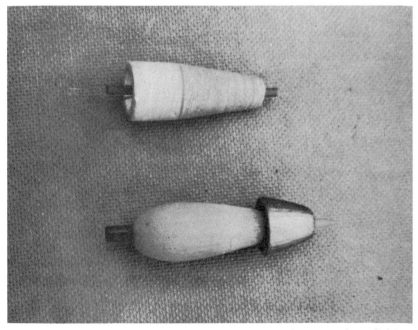

Popping corks such as these are popular in salt-water bay fishing in southern states. Float at top is made of molded plastic and has weight molded in bottom to make it float upright. Lower float is made of cork. Weight must be attached beneath it to make it float upright. Depending upon force applied, these corks make "popping" and "chugging" sounds.

Author's daughter Laura June with a three-pound speckled trout
(spotted weakfish). She caught the fish on a live shrimp bait
fished under a popping cork. The speckled trout readily responds
to the noise made by a popping cork.

Another loner is the bobcat. It will home in on the varmint squeal because it loves to sink its teeth into a fat rabbit. But the bobcat is a woods creature. The most plaintive rabbit cry in the world is not going to pull a bobcat out into open country if there is a speck of daylight showing. This is a nocturnal creature that prowls only after dark. Any bob on the move during the daytime is one suffering from malnutrition or one that has been chased out of hiding. Furthermore, a bob is not going to cross an open prairie unless the animal is being hard pressed. The animal will work around the clearing by staying as much as possible back in the fringe thicket or woods.

In doing research for this book I wrote to Jim Olt of the P. S. Olt Co., previously mentioned pioneer company in the manufacture of wildlife calls. I listed four reasons why game responds to calls and asked for his comments. The following is what he wrote:

"To your four basic reasons why birds and animals answer a call, I would add a fifth reason—want of company. I believe this is the main reason why ducks, and probably also geese, come to calls. Ducks are especially gregarious. I've had them come to calls when their crops were full of corn and there was plenty of other water around for them to drop into. But the calling and decoy spread meant company of other ducks. This is also the theory behind a bobwhite quail call; it's used mainly to call a covey back together after it has been flushed. The same is also true of chukar partridge.

"And I sometimes suspect the reasons overlap. Like in elk calling, I believe its an anger-sex proposition. A bull will become enraged at the challenge bugle of another bull, but this is due to the sex drive of the rut. I've bugled an elk call at large herd bulls after the rut was over, and they paid little attention to the call—probably thought it was just a rambunctious little spike bull feeling his oats. That same bugle two months earlier would have driven those big bulls into a frenzy.

"Some of the reasons game responds are rather obvious. Like crows coming to a call in anger, predators coming for a meal. But predators will also respond to much more than just the screaming rabbit-in-distress of a predator call. They have been known to come to a turkey, squirrel, and quail call also. I imagine the sound of a clucking chicken would be a good call for foxes if you could get some volume.

"But the curiosity reasons why creatures respond to a call are most interesting of all. You can often get turkeys to gobble by slamming a car door. I've had deer come to a predator call in amazing fashion.

"I was antelope hunting in northwestern Wyoming a few years ago. We'd spotted a number of old bobcat tracks in the creek bottoms, and decided to do some calling at night. At several stands I had mule deer come blundering to within 25 feet, and as many as eight at one time! It was actually weird to have deer come thundering up and standing for several minutes downwind in a mild breeze trying to figure out what was making that gosh-awful sound."

Animals and birds show various moods, including playfulness, anger, fear, hunger, sex, and sociability. Fear is the one emotion that the hunter wants never to arouse in his target. A frightened animal is going to clear out of the area in a hurry. The wildlife caller causes fear when he repeatedly sounds "clinkers." Unless the game has already been hunted hard, a "clinker" or two will not cause total fear with the resulting dash for cover. The sour notes, however, will cause suspicion that could result in the game making a cautious and circumventing approach.

The varmint caller seeks to stimulate within the animal he seeks the desire to eat. This is a basic desire, and one more pronounced among predators than with other species of wildlife. The animal that answers the urge to feed is an easy one to attract, for when hunger takes over, natural caution drops. Caution, too, is thrown to the winds when creatures respond to mating and challenge calls. The mating call, of course, stimulates the sex urge, while the challenge provokes anger. When the appeal is made to curiosity, neither animals nor birds drop their natural caution. Curiosity is practically synonymous with suspicion, and a suspicious creature, whether it is an animal, bird, or man himself, is extremely cautious. So whatever call is employed, the user must project himself into the being of the game he is seeking and attempt to fathom what mood is likely to be stimulated.

Let's run down the list of creatures mentioned in this text and list reasons why they respond to calls.

Ducks—company, security, food.

Geese—company, security, food.

Quail—security, company.

Dove—company.

Turkey—company, security, sex.

Pheasant—challenge, sex.

Chukar—company, security.

Crow—anger, challenge, company, food, rescue.

Squirrel—food, anger, curiosity.

Coon—curiosity.

Fox—food.

Coyote—food.

Bobcat—food, sex.

Wolf—food.

Deer—challenge, curiosity.

Elk—sex, challenge.

Moose—sex, challenge.

Some terms like food, sex, and anger are self-explanatory. Other terms need amplification to make their meanings clear cut.

The term company simply means the animals or birds are gregarious. They are not loners, but form into groups of several to many families. Security indicates the species leans to safety in numbers. The term challenge is indicative of anger or a belligerent mood, but in the case of wildlife it is used in reference to species that regard a certain territory as their own. These are the creatures that are ready to chase off all intruders from what they consider to be their private domain.

The challenge is paramount with some species. The bull elk is going to challenge and run off every other male that poses a threat to his rule over the harem. The cock pheasant will react similarly to another cock that intrudes into its domain.

One crow will challenge another over a meal, a resting post, or spot in the roost. But let a crow get into trouble and start "ca-aawing" for help, and other crows within hearing will respond by flying to the aid of the strickened bird, and that aid will be in the form of an attack on the molester. I have had crippled crows in hand scream to the extent of bringing their brethren into the immediate vicinity. I have never had crows attack me in the true meaning of the word, but I have had them "buzz" real close. I have actually seen them attack foxes.

This "to the rescue" reaction in crows has always amazed me in the light of reactions within a gaggle of geese. Crows can fight like hell among themselves, but let one bird get in trouble and the rest of the gang will wing to its aid. Yet family ties in the crow clan are non-existent. The birds are as promiscuous as the proverbial alley cat and they don't mate for life. As soon as the young are strong enough to fend for themselves, they completely desert the mother bird. Furthermore any young that may be slow in going off on its own is likely to be chased out by the mother bird.

Geese on the other hand mate for life. The young stay with the parent birds for a year, sometimes longer. As strong as the family ties are, however, the adults in a gaggle will never go back to a stricken juvenile calling for help. An adult will stay in the general vicinity of its fallen mate, but not as close as to make itself an in-range target. In the case of a fallen juvenile, parent desertion will be absolute and final. Yet there is a curious thing about the juvenile's attachment to its parents. When I mention juveniles, I am not referring to the downy little goslins but to the immature birds that are fully plumaged and are able to make the long migration flights. Parental concern over the flightless goslins is something else. Any creature that threatens the safety of a goslin is going to have a real fight with the parent birds.

Skilled goose hunters know the secret of culling a complete limit of birds from a single gaggle. It is a case of shooting the adult or leader birds. Juveniles, especially snow and blue geese, place so much trust in the fallen leader—or perhaps they are really confused in not having a pace-setter ahead—that they will mill round and round over the downed adult. Frequently the hunter will have ample time to reload his gun and blast down more geese before the remaining birds move out of range. Even then if the surviving birds are juveniles, they are likely to circle high over the area for quite a length of time. And oh how they call, seemingly pleading and begging for parental guidance.

Except for certain predators and a few wildlife species that are loners by nature, most species tend strongly to mingle with their own kind. It is not that all members of a specific species are agreeably sociable, but it is more a case of numbers for survival.

Every form of wildlife preys upon weaker forms of life. Consequently the weaker the species, the more apt its members are to congregate. To illustrate, the lone bobwhite quail is far more likely to fall victim to a fox, weazel, or hawk than the same bird would be if in a covey of a dozen birds. Note how quail rest at night—in a circle with each bird facing out. It is a defense for mutual protection. Pioneers crossing the Indian country in our early history used the identical pattern in circling their wagons at the end of the day's journey. It lessened the odds of any single wagon being picked off. The quail covey that is broken by a marauder is brought back together because the individual birds are able to communicate. They simply call to each other and reassemble.

17.

Time to Call

THERE IS MORE TO GAME CALLING THAN JUST MASTERING THE AP-propriate sounds. The finest duck caller in the world is not going to lure a single downy feather if he tries to do his calling in the middle of the Mojave Desert. Obviously the call is a worthless piece of junk if the user persists in trying to use it in an area that is not inhabited by or at least traveled through by the bird or game species he seeks. In short a call is useful only where the action is.

This, however, is just one part of calling. The weather, too, must be taken into consideration. Birds and beasts respond to weather in a pattern remarkably similar to that of man. They are most active when the weather is pleasant. Birds and animals generally feed at two different times during the day—from dawn until about 8 or 9 o'clock in the morning, and then again in the afternoon from about an hour or two before dusk until an hour or two after. With some species, particularly some of the cats and canines, almost all of their feeding is at night.

But feeding behavior and habits vary under different weather conditions. These differences must be taken into consideration by the wildlife caller.

On the typical warm day, the feeding period will be in the cool, early morning and late afternoon hours. If the weather is unusually hot, the feeding periods will be short. During the daylight hours between feeding periods, the game will bed down in cool, secluded spots. Consequently birds and animals react to calling far better in early morning and late afternoon than they do at midday. You can pretty well figure that any game that responds to calling during the heat of the day is one that is (1)

94

on the verge of starvation, (2) spooked from its midday resting spot, or (3) a juvenile. Calling, even expert calling, will have only limited effect on species bedded down. There are, of course, some marked exceptions. These exceptions are the predators, especially foxes, coyotes, and crows. The plaintive, mournful squeal of the crippled rabbit will stir foxes and coyotes into activity. The crow fight calls and distress calls will likewise lure the black bandits, even in the heat of the day.

On a cool day, particularly one on which the sky is heavy overcast, wildlife feeding periods are greatly extended. When browse is relatively scarce, the game may be active the entire day.

What do birds and animals do on a rainy day? The answer is simple. They do the same thing any sane, sensible human would do. They seek out shelter from the weather. This is true even with waterfowl. They may spend most of their lives in water, but this does not mean they like to fly in the rain. Any waterfowl one sees on wing during a rain storm is a bird that was frightened out of its shelter and is looking for new shelter.

Birds and animals are very active after rainy periods, with the length of activity depending upon the duration of the rain squall. A heavy rain will knock a lot of food matter out of the trees as well as cause a lot of sub-surface animal life to emerge to the surface. It makes for easy pickings for all forms of life that inhabit the wilderness. A passing rain shower is usually followed by an intensive feeding and activity period that may last for an hour. A lengthy rain period will be followed by a corresponding longer feeding and activity span. If the rain session is followed by relatively cool temperatures, the activity period may be one of day-long duration. The astute hunter can put his wildlife calling to good use in these periods that follow rain.

Wildlife has a built-in barometer that warns of weather changes, and species are able to sense the coming change many hours in advance of its actual arrival. A rising or high barometer is indicative of good weather. A low or falling barometer presages the opposite. Wildlife reacts accordingly. If the hunter would correlate his trips with barometric action, he would enjoy far better success. All birds and animals respond rather well to calling when barometric pressure is high. But when the barometer falls to storm level, no amount of calling will produce satis-factory results. The game beds down and stays put. Even the wail of the crippled rabbit won't stir predators into activity. The built-in barometer in wildlife is just nature's way of protecting the species from the elements. Without it game would become extinct.

The effectiveness of the game call is in direct relation to the force of the wind. On the dead calm day the call has what one might call 360-degree reach, meaning it can be heard equally well in all directions. This, of course, increases its effectiveness. A light wind reduces the upwind range of the call but not enough to seriously hamper its effectiveness. For example, con-sider the squirrel bark call. With a light wind the sound may carry 100 yards upwind and 150 yards downwind. But with a strong wind, its upwind reach may be reduced drastically to perhaps 50 yards. This presents no problem if you know squirrels inhabit a particular tree, but if you are hunting "blind" so to speak, you are certain to find the going rough. Don't think for a second the strong wind will carry the "bark" any great distance downwind. Its downwind range will be severely deadened and covered by wind whistling through the trees, the rustling of leaves and brush, and the creaking of limbs. Frankly trying to hunt squirrels on a blustery day is a lost cause. Not only will the sound of the call be drowned out by forest noises, the hunter will be faced with the added disadvantage of everything moving and shaking in the tree tops. Unless he has a "squirrel eye" he can look right at a bushy-tail high on a limb and never see it.

Except for waterfowl the best results in game calling can be had on a dead calm or light breezy day. On such a day the caller has around-the-compass reach, although the hunter will be faced with a situation of having to watch all directions for responding game. Still he will have the added advantage of his scent not being picked up by the game. With no wind at all, scents tend to rise straight up before fanning out. In the case of waterfowl the windless day is a lousy one. Ducks and geese tend to raft up and will stay put until something spooks them to take wing. A few duck species, particularly the mallard, are willing to va-cate a placid pond in response to good calling on the windless day.

Survival in the wild as far as game is concerned is survival of the fittest. Except for extremely large mammals like bears or the larger of the predators—wolves and coyotes—there is always something bigger around to prey on each species of bird and animal. The frisky squirrel that cavorts around the base of a tree on a windless day is one nervous cat when the wind is up. The animals will move with extreme caution, pausing frequently to sniff for scent of an intruder and eyeball the surroundings. A dead limb breaking off a tree and tumbling to the ground will send the squirrel up its tree with jet-like speed. After all, the squirrel does not know if the limb was broken off by the wind or under the weight of some predator. And where possible danger lurks, quick retreat is always a safe course to take. The same is true with deer. These animals will browse at ease on a dead calm day, but when the wind rises, the same animal will do more looking and listening than actual browsing. If the wind reaches a point where the deer figures it has no margin of safety, the animal will retreat to an area where it can bed down with a reasonable degree of security. Attempting to call deer under strong wind conditions is like trying to light a cigarette in a hurricane.

A foggy day is a poor one for any kind of game calling. Fog seriously impairs all of an animal's senses—sight, hearing, and smell. These are the animal's very keys to survival. When these senses are impaired, it is only natural instinct for the game to remain close to the sanctity of its den. This all adds up to meaning that game moves little on a foggy day.

Fogs produce some curious things in regard to sound. Sometimes it will mute sounds; other times it will greatly magnify sound.

I have hunted ducks in fogs and been sprinkled with spent pellets, yet I was barely able to hear the report of the gun that fired the shots. Yet on a clear day that same shotgun would sound like a baby cannon. I recall one duck hunt where three parties were involved. The blinds were about a quarter-mile apart. I was in the middle blind. In spite of the heavy fog the ducks flew like flying was going out of style. When they saw the decoys, they came in with the same reckless abandon. For an hour or so there was a steady cannonade. I swore to my companion that there were poachers on both sides of us and just out of sight of our blind. The roar of the shooting was almost deafening. Yet when the fog lifted there was not a soul between our blind and the other two. The fog did it all, and what a fog will do to gun shots it will also do to calling.

18.

Role of Movement

IMMOBILITY MORE THAN CAMOUFLAGE IS OF UTMOST IMPORTANCE where animals and birds are concerned. Except for the primates, all animals are unable to distinguish colors. The world around them registers from white through all shades of gray to black. As long as the hunter does not outline his shape, he can get away with wearing pink pants, a yellow shirt, and a red cap. All of these colors will appear to the animal in shades of gray. Then if the hunter has something behind him—tree, brush, or high grass—to keep his shape from silhouetting, he can do very nicely with a game call. But this is true only as long as he remains very still. He can get away with a few moves as long as they are slow. Sudden moves attract attention and will spook game.

Some species of wildlife can distinguish colors. These are mainly birds. Their gay plumage, especially that of the males, stands out most vividly during the mating season. Look to the ducks as an example. Ducks will veer off from hunters clothed in loud colors. I have hunted ducks for more than 30 years, and I have been on too many hunts where the birds shied away from a blind because one of the occupants wore a bright cap that did not blend in with the background. On one occasion my partner wore a bright neon red cap. Flight after flight of ducks worked almost into range and then shied off. Temper got the best of me and I grabbed the boy's cap and threw it under the seat in the blind. It made him angry because there was a slight drizzle, but his anger completely vanished when birds began to work to my calling and came in close for cinch shots. He learned his lesson so well that when we quit hunting, he took the cap out from under the seat and stomped it down into the mud.

When a hunter uses a game call, he must at all times be extremely careful to remain as inconspicuous as possible. He must always keep in mind that his presence in the wild is foreign to the creatures that inhabit the area. Animals and birds have had enough contact with man to recognize him as a source of danger.

The trophy deer or elk did not get that way because the animal disregarded the presence of man. Quite likely some place in the animal's life it had a frightening experience with man and learned to recognize him as a threat to its existence. A hunter skilled in rattling deer antlers is not going to pull a prize buck within range if he (the hunter) stands out in the middle of an open field. Any animals he lures are certain to be young ones that have not yet learned that man himself is the most dangerous of all.

The hunter who uses a call to locate his game and then stalk it is in a far less critical situation than the fellow who seeks to attract his game. Nevertheless, the stalk hunter must be careful not to make foreign noises or sudden movements in his approach to the game. He must utilize to the fullest every available bit of cover. He will be approaching game alerted only to the fact that another animal of the same species is in the general vicinity. The stalked animal may be eyeballing the direction from which the sound of the game call came, but the hunter has an advantage of mobility to make his approach from another direction.

The other fellow using the attraction call and seeking to bring the game to him faces all sorts of complications. With some species he may have to do repeated calling to keep the game working his direction. Meanwhile all the time the animal or bird is trying to pinpoint the exact location of the call. Consequently, if the hunter is to be successful in pulling the game within gun range, he must be hidden well and remain as still as a dead mackerel. He must look *through* the cover of his hide and not over it.

Then the closer the game works, the more careful he must be in the use of the call. A single sour or false note is not likely to alert game a quarter mile away. That same sour "clinker" sounded with the game a hundred yards out is almost certain to alarm the game to the point of spooking.

The volume used to reach the animal a quarter-mile off is too much when the game is out only a hundred yards. The hunter must keep in mind that the closer the game comes, the more he must mute his call to tone down volume. Every now and then, and especially for kicks, some expert callers will work their calls even after the target is in range just to see how close they can pull the game. The average hunter, however, will be far more satisfied and put more game in his bag if he will be content just to pull the target within effective gun range. Chances of attracting game to within "spitting distance" are extremely remote. The pros can do it with a degree of consistency, but in the case of the average hunter it is purely coincidental.

It becomes even more complicated when the game called is at a level higher than the hunter, such as in the case of hunting waterfowl. From its altitude the duck or goose has the distinct advantage. At ground level the brush between the caller and the game is usually adequate to screen the hunter. The waterfowl caller must be careful not to make any moves, and he must keep his face hidden as much as possible behind the reeds and grass that make up his blind.

He knows that the waterfowl will make its final approach to the decoys by coming into the wind. But before swinging into that final approach, the duck or goose—unless it is a young and immature bird—will do a lot of circling and wheeling. The fowl may make several 360-degree circles around the entire area before swinging to the decoys. This can be a most trying time for the hunter.

He must put the brakes on the normal reaction to turn his head to keep the bird in sight. Any head turning is likely to be picked up by the birds, and it is almost certain then they will vacate the area. It is generally accepted among better waterfowlers that when the birds swing behind the hunter and are out of sight, the only justified call then is a light feeding chuckle. Anything more than that is likely to pinpoint the exact location of the caller.

Fortunately for the wildlife caller most species of game do not scrutinize the layout as thoroughly as waterfowl. Take the fellow calling foxes, coyotes, etc. These animals are likely to come in from any direction, but when they do respond, they come straight in toward the source of the call. They don't wheel and figure eight the area as do waterfowl.

Being inconspicuous to the game is more than just donning a camouflage suit to blend in with the terrain. The camouflage is of little value if the user is unable to remain still. Many a deer hunter has looked straight at a trophy buck in the fringe of a thicket and still failed to see the animal. The deer is one of many species of wildlife that can stand absolutely motionless for long periods of time.

In this connection a memorable deer hunt comes to mind. It was memorable because the only fellow in the party who came within easy range of a buck walked right by the animal and never saw it.

There were two of us in a tree blind in central Texas. Nothing came within even long range of our blind. We glassed every inch of the area and saw not a flicker. Then we picked up an animal browsing on the edge of an open field at the far end of the valley. The range was a good half-mile, and it was pointless to ever consider a shot. Se we just watched the animal browse and hoped that by some outside chance it might wander in our direction. Then suddenly the deer became quite alert, raising its head and ears. A few seconds later it stepped cautiously into the fringe of the thicket that bordered the field. The animal appeared to be watching something off to one side.

Off to the left I noticed movement in the thicket. A few seconds later out stepped a member of our hunting party, his red hunting jacket standing out in bold contrast to the surrounding terrain. We figured the fellow had sighted the deer and was working around for a clear shot. But instead of stalking the animal, the red-coated figure crossed the open meadow and vanished into the thicket on the other side. The buck remained motionless the whole time, and after the hunter vanished, the deer turned around and bounded out of sight.

Later back at the hunting camp we asked the hunter why he did not shoot the animal. He could not have been more than a hundred yards from where the deer was standing. The fellow angrily insisted he eyed the area thoroughly and that there was never a deer there at any time. Yet two of use watched the entire episode through eight-power glasses and at one time cross-haired the animal in a ten-power rifle scope. The truth of the matter is the deer stood so still that it blended in perfectly with the thicket. In crossing the field our hunting buddy may have looked right at the animal a half dozen times without ever seeing it.

The point of the whole story is that if the wildlife caller can be as still as that deer, the fellow will be certain to have success with his call.

Fortunately for wildlife, man is a restless creature. He lacks the ability, willpower, or whatever else it takes to become like a stone. He always has to scratch his nose—or behind. Instead of moving his eyes from side to side, he turns his entire head. He crosses and uncrosses his legs. And on and on it goes. Every time he moves he attracts the attention of some of the wildlife in the area. Perhaps he noticed the shrill "cawk" of a bluejay high up in the tree or the raucous "caw" of the crow perched atop the dead tree in the middle of the clearing. If the hunter's knowledge of wildlife lore was complete, he would wince at the truth of the matter. The bluejay and crow are the bane of hunters. They are quick to note a strange, out-of-character movement or flicker, and they are just as quick to sound warning cries. They alert everything else in the vicinity that something is amiss.

After reading this chapter test yourself on your ability to remain still. Make it an easy test, like reclining back in an easy chair in a quiet room. The only movements not to be charged against you will be those involving the eyes. Have a friend mark down every other movement you make in the space of five minutes. The results should deflate your ego.

The story of being inconspicuous is more than blending with the foliage and remaining motionless. Man has body odor. When he is dating the gals around town, he can kill this odor with a wide assortment of deodorants, hair oils, after-shave lotions, and colognes. This sweet-smelling stuff may flutter the hearts of his dates, but they will only put fright into the hearts of wild game for these smells are foreign to them.

Still man's odor must be neutralized or at least minimized when hunting. There are today a number of commercially produced scents to use. Some are game-attracting scents that can be sprinkled around your blind. These are rather musky and unpleasant to smell as far as man is concerned. Thanks to modern chemistry there are others not so unpleasant that can be put on your hunting clothes.

The very worst thing a wildlife caller can do is to smoke at his hunting stand. There is the motion of his hand moving the cigarette to and from his lips. There is the motion in the cloud of smoke itself. Far worse are the smoke and tobacco odors that cling to the area and permeate the air. The scent of smoke strikes fear in all wildlife, including the largest of mammals. If you have any doubts about how offensive smoke is to animal life, note how the pet dog or cat ambles to the far side of the room when you light up a smoke.

The reaction of wild game is far more pronounced. Some years back I used to visit a rancher who had several caged bobcats and foxes. The animals had been caged long enough so that they would not snarl or make menacing gestures when a human neared their cages. But we were interested in noting their reactions to smoke. We lit up cigars and blew smoke at the cages. Each animal went into a frenzy, screaming and howling and clawing to break out of their pens. Their eyes reflected terror. The wild animal in the forest that gets a whiff of smoke reacts similarly and bolts helter skelter in the opposite direction.

The important thing to remember in wildlife calling is that you are seeking to bring game to your immediate area—an area that you contaminate with movement, sounds, and smells completely foreign to the surroundings. If you fail to minimize these "foreign elements," you will not have much success in calling.

19.

Concealment

THROUGHOUT THIS BOOK THE READER WILL FIND FREQUENT REFER-
ences to and remarks about concealment. The close reader will
even discover that the same points concerning the subject may
be mentioned two or three times. Why then this repetition? It
is done simply to drive the points home, for concealment in
hunting is what oxygen is to breathing.

So many folks misconstrue the meaning of concealment. They
believe if they get BEHIND something they are hidden. This is
true but only so long as they remain behind the object. Concealment is lost when they look over or around it.

Why?

Whether one looks over the object or from one side of it, his
head—and if he sticks out far enough, his shoulders, too—presents a silhouette not in keeping with the general surroundings.
If there is movement in either head or shoulders, it is often
enough to attract the attention of the animal or bird. The creature may not recognize you immediately as man, but it is certain
to consider the strange silhouette as something suspicious. If
someone has taken a recent pot shot at the creature, it is certain
to take off for parts far removed. Even if it has not been shot
at recently, the animal will bolt if the strange silhouette moves.

With creatures that see colors only as varying shades of gray,
the hunter can often conceal himself better by getting in front
of the object. This is particularly true if he happens to be wearing camouflage clothing. The outdoorsman in the camouflaged
gear can even keep himself reasonably concealed from creatures
having the ability to distinguish colors. This is quite true with
birds as long as the hunter manages to keep his face well

screened. Keep in mind that almost all species of birdlife can distinguish colors and see them in their true hues. If the hunter wears a red jacket and a yellow cap, he is going to be recognized quickly as an enemy by any bird that may see him. All of the four-legged animals see colors only in varying shades of gray, ranging from snow white to coal black. The hunter with the red jacket and yellow cap can escape detection if he remains perfectly still, for the animal will see the red as a very dark gray and the yellow as a light gray.

The outdoorsman who sits, stands, or kneels with the tree trunk, boulder, or bush to his back can escape detection as long as he does not move or silhouette himself in strong light. If he is wearing camouflaged clothes, the color blind animal may view him as brush or a mound of weeds. To the same color blind creature the red jacket-yellow cap fellow can be mistaken for a boulder or a stump in front of the tree. The important thing is to remain absolutely still.

The competent outdoorsman, whether he hunts with game call or not, uses the landscape to his advantage. A straight line may be the shortest distance between two points, but this old dodge can get a fellow into a heap of trouble. The straight line from where he steps out of his car to where he plans to hunt may carry him well out into the open where he can be seen clearly by all the wildlife in the area. The same hunter will be far better off taking the long way around, always observant and careful to keep himself as inconspicuous as possible. It may take a half-hour longer to reach his hunting blind, but it will be time well spent if he does not alert wildlife that there is danger in the area.

Where game of considerable size is concerned and especially with species whose normal range may cover vast spaces, the hunter should approach his blind into the wind. If he approaches from upwind, he is certain to leave a scent that game will pick up well before it comes within hunting range. This must be kept in mind where such game as deer, elk, wolves, coyotes, and foxes are concerned. These animals may roam from several miles to scores of miles a day, depending upon how plentiful food is in a given area.

In the case of such creatures as squirrels, the into-the-wind and behind-the-cover approach to the hunting stand is without merit. The normal range of the squirrel is a matter of just a few acres. The only times when squirrels move great distances is when an acute food shortage exists. The approach into squirrel territory should be made with as little commotion and attention as possible. Any alarm the hunter may cause by his approach can be cancelled out if when he takes his stand, he remains still and quiet for about 15 minutes. This is ample time for the animals to overcome their initial fright or suspicion. Then after that 15-minute wait, the hunter can go to work with his squirrel call.

A good rule of thumb in seeking out concealment in the woods or brush is to work in the shadows. In rolling plains or hill country stay off the ridges to avoid silhouetting. When the sun is low in the sky keep in the shadows as much as possible. Remember your body can cast quite long shadows when the sun is at a small angle to the horizon. A shadow that moves can cause an animal to bolt.

Movement around water areas presents several problems. The hunter on the shoreline of a lake can stand out in bold relief to the animal eyeballing him from a few yards back in the thicket. In spite of the fact that water is necessary to sustain life, animals approach water with unusual caution, for more danger lurks around the proverbial waterhole than any other place in either the woods or the prairies. The waterhole is the natural place for ambush. Only young, immature animals or those crazed by thirst approach water without caution. The older animals, the trophy ones, approach water with the same care a mother shows in sending junior to his first day at school. The rule of thumb for the hunter here is to stay well back into the thicket when skirting around a lake or pond.

The waterfowl hunter usually approaches his blind and nestles himself in it well before the first crack of dawn. Since ducks and geese do all their traveling by air, the hunter is not faced with a problem of leaving a scent. Furthermore, the hunter's movements to the blind are screened since they are carried out before first light. So he need not take the long way around. He can follow the shortest distance, that straight line.

He is only fooling himself. That straight-line path day after day from auto to blind leads only to the well-worn, beaten path. This path when viewed from the sky, which happens to be the point of view for ducks and geese, can stand out like a traffic light. In heavily gunned regions, this path alone can be enough to cause birds to shy off. Even good calling won't compensate.

In the matter of concealment the bird caller faces a situation far more critical than that faced by the game caller who is usually in a blind on the same level with the animal he seeks. The bird caller, and especially in the case of ducks and geese, must be particularly careful not to needlessly expose his face. The upturned face, even on a dismal day, can pick up light and stand out like a beacon. And if that face happens to be wearing glasses—wow!

Since birds are able to distinguish colors, the camouflage suit is an absolute must. The fellow with the red jacket and yellow cap is going to spook birds long before they ever get into gun range. Even in a well-constructed blind these bright colors are likely to reveal the hunter's presence for the simple reason that ducks and geese scrutinize a decoy thoroughly before setting their wings. Waterfowl usually make at least one complete circle around the area, and this means the decoy rig and the surrounding landscape, which includes the hunting blind, will get the eyeball treatment from 360 degrees. And if the birds are spooky, they may make three or four circles. If that red jacket or yellow cap shows through the foliage at the wrong time, the hunter will never get the birds to work into effective range.

If the waterfowl hunter is to be successful, he must have protective covering from all sides, he must wear clothing that blends with the vegetation, and he must expose his face as little as possible. A few waterfowlers I know use lampblack or theatrical paint to do their faces up jungle style. Others drape nets over their heads. Both methods are acceptable, but personally I feel these methods are a lot of extra work when it is so easy to get the job done by developing good habits in the blind.

The basic habit is one looking THROUGH the cover and not OVER it or AROUND it. Move your face right up to the vegetation and look right through it. If you focus your eyes on distant objects, and flying ducks and geese are such, it is easy. Let your eye wander to a single blade of grass or stalk of cane a foot from your face and you are in trouble. The secret is in focusing on distant objects. Then you just sort of "look through" any blade of grass or cane stalk that may wave in front of one eye or the other.

20

Materials for Calls

CALLING ANIMALS AND BIRDS TO LURE THEM INTO THE TRAPPER'S snares or within range of the hunter's weapons is as old as hunting itself. Although there are no records or visible evidence around to support it, the earliest caveman probably used an assortment of grunts, groans, and whistles to lure his intended victim within killing range of the crude weapons of his day.

Letters, diaries, and histories of our colonials and then later our frontiersmen contain references, often sketchy and lacking in details, of animals and birds being attracted by sounds.

Game calling is perhaps best documented in the history of waterfowling. Early writings of waterfowling in Europe contain references to "tolling" ducks and geese. In this case the calling was done with tame ducks and geese expressly trained to lure their kin to doom.

The earliest of calling was the product of lungs, vocal cords, and how one pursed his lips. As man gained knowledge, he took to fashioning instruments that would make calling easier. The earliest instruments were crudely made from the horns and bones of animals. Then as man became more skilled in the use of tools and as new tools were invented, later calls were carved from various materials, usually wood, and then fitted together.

Since the pioneer's existence depended upon his skill to bag game consistently, he took the time and patience to learn as much as possible about the predominant game that inhabited the area. He learned the sounds of wildlife, and he could immediately identify the species. He then used his knowledge to make the appropriate sounds to lure the creatures within range of his weapons.

Today we have three types of calls—the one that is blown, the hand operated, and the electronic. With some species of animals and birds, all three types can be used. With other species, especially migratory waterfowl, only two can be employed. The third, the electronic call, is outlawed. Electronic duck and goose calls, transistorized and operated by batteries, are real symphonies. These records and tapes carry the calls and sounds of a concentration of birds, rather than just one. With waterfowl populations hovering only slightly above the danger mark as it is, these electronic devices are far too effective to be put into the hands of every hunter. The electronic waterfowl call can practically guarantee the user the limit of birds. If every waterfowler used such a device, the waterfowl population would be reduced to such a low level that hunting would have to be banned. Consequently for conservation purposes the electronic call is banned for waterfowl hunting.

Whether a call is for waterfowl, crows, varmints, etc., one can find instruments made of wood, molded plastic, pliable plastic, soft rubber, hard rubber, and metal. And, of course, there are instruments that combine several of the materials mentioned.

Most of the hand-operated "squeakers" are made of soft rubber or pliable plastic. By far those manufactured of rubber are the best, especially when the desired calls are a series of rapid squeaks. Rubber is resilient enough to permit rapid operation. Pliable plastic will produce the same tones, but you can't get the same rapid sequence that the soft rubber device offers. The plastic, of course, will last for years, while the rubber is prone to deteriorate due to moisture, dry rot, heat, etc., in a few years. These calls are inexpensive, and I would rather buy a new rubber call every three or four years and be sure of getting the sounds I desire rather than purchase the so-called "lifetime" plastic call that does not operate quite so effectively. The difference between the soft rubber and pliable plastic calls are most dramatically pointed up in cold weather, when this kind of plastic has a tendency to get quite stiff.

I own duck and goose calls made of wood, molded plastic, hard rubber, and metal. I can attract waterfowl with all of them. Nevertheless, each has its advantages and disadvantages, and as long as I am aware of these factors, I can accomplish what I set out to do—that is, to call ducks and geese. The instruments made of wood or hard rubber produce the most realistic sounds under all conditions. Molded plastic calls, unless the walls are thick, sound far too harsh. They can cause real problems on a quiet, windless day. On a windy day, however, there are enough resulting marsh noises to take the harshness out of the thin-walled plastic call. Metal calls often have a "tinny" sound and some models have a distinct "ring." Many waterfowlers find the "ring" and "tinny" noises objectionable.

Good waterfowl calls must be rugged in order to stand abuse and all sorts of disagreeable weather. The wood and hard rubber models stand up rather well. Metal calls are subject to rust, especially when used around salt water, and they are profuse "sweaters" under some temperature conditions. It would be okay if the moisture collected only on the *outside* of the instrument. Unfortunately it collects inside as well, and moisture on the sounding reed will result in the call sounding half "quack" and half "squeal." And this sound is unwaterfowl-like to say the least. The molded plastic calls are prone to falling apart in cold weather. It is most embarrassing to grab your call and discover the trumpet end has fallen off.

Does all this mean plastic and metal are poor materials for wildlife calls? Not at all. It may hold true for waterfowl calls, but in other aspects of calling either molded plastic or metal may be superior to wood and hard rubber.

For example, I have a half dozen quail calls, including one of metal and another of molded plastic. All of the calls are workable, but the metal one is far superior. The molded plastic ranks next, while the remaining wood or hard rubber calls run third. Wood and hard rubber seem to mute the shrill, distinct whistle of the bob white and have far less range than the metal whistle.

Good game and bird calls have something in common with gunstocks. We live in an age of super synthetics and in spite of the fact that many of the synthetics are practically wearproof, wood is still used in the manufacture of some items. Take gunstocks as examples. They have been made successfully from synthetics and they serve the purpose extremely well. In spite of this all of the fine guns are stocked with walnut. Or for that matter note the wall coverings in the den. It, too, is made of wood.

Whether it is the den wall, a gunstock, or a game call, wood is the material of manufacture because of its beauty. I have yet to see a synthetic match the exquisite beauty of highly polished fine hardwood. Hardwoods like teak, Brazilian rosewood, cocobolo, cherry, and black walnut are outstanding for the manufacture of excellent game calls, both in quality and appearance. One must, of course, expect to pay a correspondingly higher price for these instruments than for similar calls mass produced from molded plastic.

Regardless of the material used in the manufacture of the instrument, it behooves the prospective buyer of any wildlife call to test the instrument in the field. It is impossible to determine either its range or the quality of the sound produced when the device is used within the confines of the sporting goods store or in a canyon walled with steel and concrete skyscrapers. All the concrete and steel jungle does is to distort sound.

21.

Electronic Calls

A NUMBER OF YEARS AGO I ACCOMPANIED A WATERFOWL BIOLOGIST into the marshes in the interest of waterfowl studies. He was concerned with banding birds and was doing a study on duck attraction with calls. He was skilled in the use of calls, and he knew what he could do with the usual mouth call. His experiment, however, centered around using a long-playing record containing the feeding gabble and contented chuckles of a large flock of ducks rather than just a single bird.

He used a battery-powered record player and amplification system. The device was rigged so that when the record was completed, the needle flipped back to the start again. This was back in the days before cartridges and long-playing tapes.

He set the device in a stand of cane and quill grass near the edge of a marsh pond. There were neither decoys nor ducks on the pond. He put the machine into operation, and we backed off into some cover about 40 yards away to await developments. The sounds that wafted back to us were perfect. In the space of about 15 minutes several dozen ducks—mallards, teal, and baldpates—flew in to the pond. In a half hour there must have been a hundred ducks either on the pond or milling in the sky above it.

Findings from a single experiment or field trip can not be accepted as valid proof positive. I accompanied the biologist on three or four more trips, and he made at least a half dozen more by himself. Every time the results were the same. Ducks poured in like salt out of a shaker. Obviously the electronic call was a whopping success. Apparently a lot of other experiments along this same line were made elsewhere because today it is illegal to hunt waterfowl with any type of electronic calling device.

A number of battery-powered calling devices are on the market today for varmint, crow, and turkey hunting. In addition to being calling devices, some of the instruments are also equipped to record wildlife sounds. They come complete with sets of recording mikes and remote controls so the hunter can set the device up in a likely spot and then move back to a vantage point to watch. Then when the game moves near a hidden mike, the device is put into operation, and the hunter has the real McCoy sounds on his tape. All he has to do then is take the contraption to where he plans to hunt and press the "play" button to be in business. And I mean one gets into business. You can get results that will be downright fantastic.

I know a couple of characters—their names won't be mentioned because I strongly suspect that they interpret game laws to suit their desires—who have gotten some excellent tapes on turkeys. They are great turkey hunters, but I don't think the birds they bag are so large as to supply *that* many turkey dinners in the course of a year. I suspect these fellows shoot over the legal limit.

A west Texas rancher who was plagued with coyote raids trapped some rabbits. He staked two of them to the ground and then injured them to make them scream and cry. All of these sounds were taped, and the tape in turn was used in his electronic varmint call. The call is so realistic and effective that he has had coyotes—also foxes—come in on the dead run. In fact, they have bolted out of the brush so fast that he finally took to using a shotgun to cut down on misses.

I have been a party to crow shoots on which recordings and tapes were used to lure the birds within range. Oh, what slaughters! A few such hunts sound terrific, and I firmly believe that when some species of wildlife become so abundant as to become pests and upset the balance of nature in a given area, corrective measures are necessary. Real sportsmen are far more than just good hunters. They are also conservationists. They know how much game can be taken from an area without any harm being done to the brood stock. Unfortunately all good hunters are not also good sportsmen, and these are the guys who penalize all of us.

These fellows are skilled in the way of wildlife and they consistently bag game. But they also over-kill. And this can upset rather delicate balances in nature. If all the hawks are eliminated from a given locale, the territory will soon be overrun with field mice. If a range is cleaned of coyotes, the area soon becomes over-populated with rabbits. And so it goes on and on.

I have hunted with sportsmen who used electronic calls, but they used them with discrimination and not as a means for wholesale slaughter. This book is not designed to promote the sales of wildlife calls. Its purpose is to inform the hunter how he can make his sport more enjoyable and rewarding by augmenting his day in the field with a wildlife call. Personally if I had my druthers, I would ban the use of electronic calls except for specific cases where it is necessary to bring certain game or bird populations under control. Electronic calls are far, far too effective, and there are far, far too many hunters who are not good sportsmen. They shoot, shoot, shoot today and care not a damn for what tomorrow may hold. When fox, coyote, or crow populations are extremely high for a given territory and other native wildlife species suffer unduly from these predators, then I can see a need for electronic calls.

Any ten-year-old child can be taught to perform the manual functions to put the electronic call into operation. Unless an area is sterile, the game will respond. It is like shooting fish in a barrel.

But it takes skill and wildlife knowledge to get results with the mouth or hand call. It is a lot like fishing. There is always a greater thrill in catching a fish on an artificial lure than on natural bait. The natural live bait attracts the fish all on its own. The artificial lure will not attract a thing unless the fisherman knows how to impart the right action to make the plug, spoon, or jig act like something that will interest the fish. Hence when you catch a fish on an artificial lure, you know you have accomplished something. My feelings parallel fishing when it comes to using manually operated wildlife calls as opposed to electronic devices. If the electronic boys take offense to my feelings, that is just their tough luck.

22.

On-the-Spot Calls

WILDLIFE CALLS COME IN A WIDE RANGE OF PRICES. DISREGARDING the electronic calls where prices can be considerable, a good hand-operated call or a mouth call can be purchased for less than five dollars. But let's suppose a fellow does not have a spare five-spot, or suppose he is out in the field and loses his call. Neither misfortune is reason for catastrophe. Any woodsman who can identify the calls of various species of wildlife and in turn has the ingenuity to recreate these sounds can use a number of objects as materials for making on-the-spot calls. They may not be nearly as effective as commercial calls but in a pinch they will produce results.

For example, any number of the rubber bulb "squeaker" toys that toddlers play with will get results in varmint hunting. The "squeak" made by the toy is a pretty good imitation of a rabbit squeal in distress. The toy won't work in open country where volume is necessary to reach distant animals, but it can be quite effective in the woods or thick brush. Another excellent close-range varmint call, especially where the fox is concerned, entails no monetary outlay whatsoever. The call is made simply by "kissing" the back of your hand. Moisten your lips well and draw out the "kiss." It is also a good imitation of a suffering rabbit. Still in the line of attracting the varmints, there is the old Indian trick of "squeaking" blades of grass. Two blades are pressed together and held firmly with the thumb and forefinger of each hand. When the edges are brought to the lips and you blow briskly, you get an excellent "squeak." The nice thing about this "squeak" is that it has considerably longer range than either the toddler's toy or the back-of-the-hand "kiss."

117

In the earlier chapter on squirrel calling, I mentioned the trick of rustling nuts in a sack to get bushy-tails to stick their heads out in the open.

There is a way to get that squirrel "bark" by using a few items you are likely to have in your pants pocket. Had it not been for a foul-up, I never would have learned this trick. It happened on a hunt when I accidentally dropped my squirrel call in the mud and then to complicate matters stepped on it. It was then that the farmer who was hunting with us came up with the coin trick. He used two silver half dollars. He put one coin in the palm of his hand and then struck the flat side of it rapidly with the edge of the other coin.

"Reckon that sounds like an old bushy barking."

He made his remark sound half-question, half-order. The coin trick worked and he got squirrels to respond, although in all fairness it must be pointed out the range of the sound is so limited that it is effective only on animals in trees in the immediate vicinity. The commercial squirrel call has sufficient reach to lure in bushy-tails from 150 to 200 yards away. The coin "barks" sound best when made with a pair of half dollar pieces. Quarters will work in a pinch but smaller coins produce too much metallic click. Don't attempt the trick with two coins of different sizes. A quarter struck against a half dollar, or a nickel against a quarter, produces a "tick" instead of a "bark."

Squirrel "barks" can be produced by striking two walnut halves—hollow to hollow—together. Still another call trick is to click your tongue against the roof of your mouth. The dry cough so prevalent in chain smokers will also fetch squirrels if the animals have not been hunted to any extent.

What would you do if on a squirrel hunt you came upon a bayou and noted bushy-tails working in the trees on the opposide side? Why, cross the bayou, of course. But suppose the bayou is too deep to cross, what then? Again, taking a situation of having no commercial call, there is a trick you can use to get the animals to find a way to cross over to you.

Wherever there is mast you will find squirrels. They love to feed on nuts, and when mast is falling, they often throw their usual caution to the wind. The trick is one that works only on a still, windless day. Gather up a good supply of nuts. Get well hidden and then start thumb-flipping nuts, one or two at a time, into the branches of a nearby tree. Squirrel ears are super sensitive to the sound of falling mast. There is the "twick" and "click" of nuts as they hit leaves and tree limbs. Then there is the most seductive sound of all when the nuts strike the ground. On dry ground the sound is a "plick"; on wet ground it is a "plat." None of these sounds are very loud, but there is nothing phony about them, and oh how they stimulate the bushy-tails. They are sounds that won't fall on deaf ears.

The bayou may be too deep for you to cross, but a greedy and hungry squirrel will find a way. I have seen the creatures work along a bank until they found tree limbs overhanging the bayou enough so they could leap across. I have seen them cross a bayou hopping from log to log to log. And on two occasions I watched squirrels swim across. The two swimmers, however, were only skin and bones animals that obviously took to the water because they were half starved. Neither animal was fit to eat, and if I ever encounter swimming bushy-tails again, they will get safe passage.

Veteran deer hunters use the same "nut trick" to get their targets out of the brush for an open shot. Deer, too, love to feed on mast. The sound of falling nuts will cause a deer to move out of its cover. This trick is not used to "call" deer in the true sense of calling. It comes into play when the hunter has located his buck but can't shoot because the animal is behind heavy brush. Then the nuts are flipped out to cause the animal to move out so the hunter can get a clear shot. The mark of a tyro deer hunter is that of attempting to bag the deer by shooting through the brush. Some bucks are killed that way, but far more escape, sometimes sorely wounded, because a twig deflected a high-speed bullet off point of aim. If you have to shoot through heavy brush, then use a rifle that shoots a heavier but lower velocity bullet. This kind of bullet will break and tear through tangle and still hit point of aim. If the brush is exceedingly dense and the ranges are short, the weapon to use then is the shotgun charged with buckshot. In respect to the shotgun, however, check the game laws for some areas prohibit the use of shotguns for deer hunting.

In addition to using calls to locate and attract game, there are times when sounds are used to stop game and make it present itself as a better target. These totally foreign sounds will bring an animal to a complete halt for a few seconds while it tries to figure out what made the strange noise. Then the creature will bolt and get out of the area pronto. At very best these sounds give the hunter—if he is alert—just enough time to line up the sights and get off a shot.

In the case of rabbits, foxes, coyotes, and deer, a shrill whistle can cause the running animal to come to a complete stop and look back. It won't be for long, but for a few seconds the hunter will have a stationary target. Although the shrill whistle won't stop running game every time, it works often enough to make the trick worthwhile. After all, the odds of scoring on a stationary target are far better than those of hitting running game.

Water is a necessity of life, and the sound of splashing in a normally quiet pond, bayou, or river can spur wildlife curiosity sufficiently to get many creatures to venture into the vicinity to learn the cause of the commotion. This is a trick of little value to the hunter seeking specific game, for it will be strictly pot luck as to what species show themselves. Nevertheless it is a good thing to know should a fellow's survival depend upon finding some kind of game.

Finally there are some people who can call game without aid of gadgets or mechanical devices. These are the folks who possess well-trained vocal cords and who are able to mimic the sounds they hear in the wild.

23.

Special Tricks

THE INGENIOUS HUNTER WHO KNOWS GAME AND BIRD HABITS, LIKES, and dislikes can make a wildlife call do things the manufacturer may never have visioned.

To illustrate the point, let me cite the case in which a crow call was used to improve a day's quail hunting. It took place in a central Texas meadow, which our host assured us was alive with fat quail. Indeed it was. The only trouble was the birds were spooky, and they kept flushing far out of gun range. If they sensed a dog within 40 or 50 feet, they would flush. Quail normally hold until the dog is just a few feet away. Often the hunter has to even kick the brush to get the birds to rise. But this was not the case with our quail that day. They were the spookiest of spooks, and they kept flushing far out of range.

Nevertheless our host was not alarmed. He simply sent his son back to the house to get his crow call. We thought he was out of his mind, but then it is not good economics to tell a host who is footing all the bills that he is crazy. We decided to let him prove that to himself.

He told us to follow the dogs. He said he would follow behind us blaring out on that confounded crow call. He was good at it. No question about that, for he soon had answering calls from the nearby woods. His crow calling also improved our quail hunting. The birds started to hold until we were almost on top of them. Even with some lousy shooting at times, we filled out our limits with ease.

Later in the morning when we returned to the ranch house, our host explained his madness. He said he thought the birds failed to hold earlier because a day or two before he had seen a fox prowling the meadow. Perhaps the fox created enough havoc to cause the birds to suspect our approaching dogs were more foxes. It made sense.

The rest of our host's explanation made sense, too. He pointed out that crows are natural enemies of quail. They eat the eggs and young in the nests, and at times will even attack mature birds. Our host pointed out that when crows are awing, quail stick close to ground cover and won't fly unless pushed.

The purpose of the automobile horn is to let the driver ahead know you want to pass, honk the wife to hurry out of the house, or to toot-toot provocatively to catch the attention of that pretty little thing on the corner. It is also an incidental tool where stalk hunting is involved.

I know of at least one case where it resulted in the bagging of a large deer and a number of cases of bagging geese. First let me tell about the deer.

An acquaintance took his wife along on a deer hunt. A morning in the hunting blind with mosquitoes all around and not a deer in sight was enough for her. She elected to spend the afternoon in the camp, promising her husband to return in the Jeep to a designated spot later in the afternoon to pick him up. She told him she would sound the horn when she returned. Along about five o'clock in the afternoon she drove to the appointed spot and started honking the horn. Although the hunting blind was less than a quarter of a mile away, the wind was wrong or something and the husband never heard the horn. Meanwhile wifey started losing her cool and honked the horn that much more.

Then she noted some sort of animal a hundred yards or so up the trail. She also noted that every time she honked the horn the animal inquisitively took a few more steps in her direction. She eventually honked the animal out into the open and noted it was a medium-size buck. She calmly slipped the rifle out of the side rack, lined up the sights, and stoned the deer with a single shot. The husband heard the shot, came to investigate, and found his wife with a big smug smile standing beside the animal. What made it worse was the fact that he had nothing to show for the day he had spent in the blind.

I don't advocate riding around honking car horns to call deer.

I merely repeat the incident to point out that occasionally some sounds, even foreign ones, will arouse enough curiosity in an animal to make it reveal its presence to the hunter.

Now to car-honking geese. This is a little stunt I have used successfully a number of times. It takes two or more hunters to make it work, and the geese must be on the ground. One hunter gets upwind of the birds. The other hunter, or hunters, go wide around the field to approach the birds from downwind. Then when the fellow upwind in the car notes his companions are in position, he starts blaring the horn. Pretty soon every goose in the gaggle will have its head erect and eyes trained on the source of the sound. The birds will be alerted to a point just short of flying. Meanwhile the companion hunters start their stalk toward the flock. It is tough for there is a lot of crawling and belly wiggling involved. And if the field is the least bit wet, it is mighty dirty going. Unless the stalkers make their presence known by noise or sudden movements, the geese will remain mesmerized enough by the horn-honking to allow the stalkers to get within jump shooting range.

In no way is this to be construed as calling game. It does not lure the game to the hunter nor does it cause the game to answer. It is simply a foreign sound that preoccupies the game's attention sufficiently so that the stalker can make a blind side approach. I have never tried it, but I would imagine you could preoccupy the attention of geese, or other game for that matter, with a clarinet, saxophone, or violin. There may be a lot of truth in the saying that music soothes the wild beast.

When it comes to wild game, I suppose some creatures are a lot like man himself. Just think back on some of the unidentifiable sounds you have heard in your life. Some instinctively repelled you. Others made you curious enough to search out the cause. The only trouble is that the line between fright and curiosity can sometimes be a thin one.

Sometimes it is an obvious and very familiar sound that gets the desired results. For example, there was the case of the rancher on the upper Texas coast. He was the victim of repeated losses of calves. Investigations indicated at least two wolves, possibly more, were getting the new-born calves. The rancher tried setting traps but got no results. He invited varmint callers to come in to see if they could rid his range of the predators. They got a few foxes and one bobcat but nary a wolf. The rancher got to wondering if perhaps the killers were rogue dogs. But he could find no dogs roaming his range.

Finally in desperation he fashioned an old cow horn into a call that sounded remarkably like a calf only a few days old. He reasoned that the predators had taken a liking to eating calves and would not stoop to anything else. He took the calf call so to speak out on the range and put his heart and soul into making sounds like a lost calf bawling for its mother. The second night he picked up some shadows lurking nearby. He and his ranch manager flicked on lights and in the glow they picked up three sets of "burning embers." They cut loose with shotguns charged with double 0 buckshot. When they examined the remains they found three red wolves. It was the end of calf losses for the rancher.

The last wolf in that particular part of Texas was supposed to have been killed some two decades earlier. The animals that took to killing livestock apparently migrated from another part of the state or perhaps even an adjacent state. They must have been pretty hungry to go after domestic livestock. Unless a wolf is on the verge of starvation, it will avoid close contact with man or anything that associates closely with man. Wolves have discovered over the years that man is dangerous game, and they have learned to stay clear of him.

All it takes is a little imagination to come up with a new trick or gimmick to fool man, animal, or bird. Many years ago a fishing guide taught me an almost sure-fire way to stir bass into action on a day when the water is dead calm. The fellow always carried a handful of B.Bs in his pocket. Every time he found a likely looking spot for bass, he would proceed to thumb-flip a few of the B.Bs high into the air. The shot struck the water with peculiar and distinctive "plips." Quite often these "plips" were followed by bass going on a feeding binge. The guide explained that the "plips" sounded much like small shiners flopping on the surface of the water. Bass take a delight in feeding on shiners, and the guide was simply employing sound to "call" the fish into action.

I have used this trick on many occasions. I have gotten results often enough to give me confidence the system has merit. But through experience I have found that only B.B-size shot produces the right "plip." Anything smaller or larger—a pebble for example—is simply a lost cause.

People sometimes refer to things that hunting and fishing guides do as being "silly." This is not so at all. If anything the folks who say "silly" are simply showing their ignorance. A guide's income depends upon his success in putting his client in game or fish. If he knows a special trick that will produce results, he will use it. If it is a means to success, it is by no means "silly."

24

Call Care and Repairs

WILDLIFE CALLS HAVE VERY FEW MOVING PARTS. THE SOUND PRO-duced by the mouth call is the result of a rapidly vibrating reed or diaphragm. With a hand-operated call the movable parts are usually handles, cranks, or hinged lids. Most people go on the assumption that the fewer the parts, the less chance there is for a malfunction. This is true until there is a malfunction, and then it is total disaster. Look at it this way, the four-cylinder engine can lose a piston and still hit on three cylinders, operating at a loss of a little more than 25 percent. The duck call has a single moving part—the reed. When that reed breaks, the loss is 100 percent. This few moving parts bit results in too many hunters mistreating wildlife calls. And then they damn the instrument when it makes a sound like a sick cat.

If that call—mouth or hand operated—is to work properly in time of need, then show it the care it so justly deserves. An inoperable squirrel call won't completely knock out a bushy-tail hunt, for you really don't need a call to hunt these little animals. A call just makes it easier. You can hunt ducks and geese without a call, too, just as long as you have some decoys showing. But when the turkey call or varmint call goes on the fritz, you have had it for the day. You can improvise and even employ some of the tricks described in the chapters on "Special Tricks" and "On-the-Spot Calls," but don't expect your hunt to be the howling success you had hoped for.

A competent outdoorsman would never think of allowing his gun to lie around gathering moisture, dirt, and rust. He treats it with care because this is the instrument of authority that puts game in his bag. The good outdoorsman shows the same care for his wildlife calls, for these are the instruments that put game within effective range of his gun.

Two musts are necessary if a game call is to make the sounds for which it is designed. It must be kept clean and it must be kept dry. Neither is easy when you consider the call is used in all kinds of weather.

Instructions that come with calls advertise most as being usable in all kinds of weather and impervious to moisture. Some hunters take this "impervious" bit literally, get their calls soaking wet, and then yowl to high heaven when the thing produces psychedelic yodels.

Out in the field a game call is handiest to reach and best protected when it is looped on a cord around your neck. The mouth call should be on a short loop, and it should hang high on one's chest. This places it in close proximity of the mouth. No long hand movements that game might see are necessary. A longer line is needed to hang the hand-operated call. It should hang about waist high. At this level the hunter seated in a blind has the call in a natural position for easy operation. The cord around the neck completely eliminates having to stuff the call in a pocket when the hunter arises to shoot.

When not in use the call should be tucked inside one's windbreaker or wet-weather gear to protect it from moisture. A wet call can be a disaster as I found out on a goose hunt. During the course of the hunt a heavy rain shower passed, and inadvertently I had failed to stuff the call inside my slicker jacket. The rain was heavy enough to thoroughly wet the inside of the call. This, too, I failed to notice. Shortly after the rain stopped, a small flock of Canada geese meandered around the field in which I had my decoys. As long as they showed interest in the decoys, I refrained from touching the call. Then the geese veered away, and I figured to change the situation with a little calling. The call, soaking wet inside, gave out a screech like a scalded alley cat—and those honkers jetted away like someone had scorched their tail feathers with a blowtorch.

It behooves the hunter to carry along a package of facial tissues. The are excellent for absorbing moisture from inside a call. It does not have to rain for a call to get wet. Your breath will put it there, too, and especially in cold weather.

A pocket will keep a call dry and protected from the elements, but experience will point up the fact that a pocket can be as inaccessible as the tightwad's wallet at dinner check time. You have to fumble to get the thing out to use it, and you have to fumble when you return it to free your hand for shooting. And then if it happens to be one of those "snakebit" days, you will completely miss the pocket and drop it in the mud or water.

During the off-season calls should be stored in dry places at room temperature, and if possible in the containers in which they were purchased. There is a hidden reason for this container bit, especially so if the call is made of wood. The wood will absorb some moisture during the season. In the six- to nine-month layoff in storage it will dry thoroughly. This means the wood will shrink ever so slightly. This shrinkage, however, is often just enough for the horn end to slip out of the trumpet end. It is embarrassing to go afield and discover you have a horn with no trumpet or a trumpet with no horn. When one is forced to take the call out of its container, one is more conscious of the parts. If the horn and trumpet fit is loose, it is a simple matter of twisting them tight again.

Calls used in a salt-laden atmosphere should be given double care when it comes time for storage. Any salt moisture that may collect on metal parts can cause enough damage to make the call totally inoperable.

After long storage the place to test a call is at home, and the time should be a couple of weeks before the hunt. Then if it does not sound right, you have ample time in which to fix or replace it.

The greatest enemies of game calls are dirt and moisture, and when put to use in the field, a call is certain to collect both.

Dirt can be cleaned out of most calls simply by tapping them sharply against the palm of your hand, or by reversing the call and blowing sharply into the trumpet end. Never tap the instrument against a hard object for the resulting jolt is likely to loosen working parts enough to radically change the pitch and/ or tone. Of course, if the call is dropped in the water or mud, then complete disassembling is necessary in order to do a proper cleaning job. Unless you know how to tone and pitch a call, it is best to leave the job to the sporting goods expert or return the instrument to the factory.

Rain and carelessness are the only reasons for moisture collecting in a hand-operated call. It is a different matter with the mouth call. Your breath carries moisture, and every time you blow the call some moisture collects. I know hunters who can blow a call all day and never wet the reed or interior. Yet I know others who can practically "soak" a call in an hour. Some folks have just more "wet breath" than others.

The moisture that collects is usually under the reed. It is trapped there simply because the seating of the reed prevents passage. This dampness can be cleared out by reversing the call and blowing very hard into the trumpet end. Under no circumstances attempt to dry the interior by inserting a handkerchief or absorbant tissue into the mouthpiece. There is always the danger of pushing too far into the instrument and hitting the reed. The pressure can bend the reed, push it too deep into its seat, or completely unseat it. The trumpet end, however, can usually be dried with a cloth or tissue without causing any damage to the reed.

Any call completely dunked in water should be wiped dry, then blown vigorously through trumpet end first, and finally allowed to dry out at room temperature. Don't ever attempt to dry the instrument in an oven. This is the way to ruin it.

25

Sound in Fishing

HAVE YOU EVER TRIED TO CALL FISH?

If your answer is "no," you have been fooling yourself. Sound is as important in fishing as it is in hunting. The wrong sound can send fish finning for the horizon. The right sound can put them on your fish stringer.

The artificial-lure fisherman uses sound as an attracting medium every time he makes a cast, which in effect is fish calling.

The plunk of the lure striking the water can turn fish away or it can attract them. If the plunk is sharp and harsh, the sound is almost certain to spook nearby fish. It may not sound loud to you, but it will to the fish for the simple reason that water is an excellent conductor of sound. Actually as far as the fish is concerned, the sound is amplified since water is five times denser than the air above.

Expert lure casters thumb their reels deftly so their artificial lures strike the water with minimum commotion. The sound is sufficiently loud to be heard or, more correctly, to be felt by fish in the vicinity, but the sound is not of such intensity as to alarm the fish.

Okay, so the initial use of sound is one of getting the fish's attention. Is there any more sound involved? Not as long as the lure rests motionless on the surface or lies still on the bottom. But as soon as the fisherman starts turning his reel handle, he begins to inject sound into the picture again.

Sounds produced by lures are aimed at arousing one of several desires within the fish. The primary desire is to feed. A secondary feeling is that of curiosity. Lures must be in motion to produce the necessary sounds, which are the results of the lure's shape and the manner in which it disturbs the surface of the water. The lure with the concave or dish-shape face will make a distinct "plop" or "chug" when jerked sharply. Both of these sounds are remarkably similar to those made by gamefish feeding on the surface. The same lure retrieved at a steady pace across the surface will cause a continuous "gurgling" sound quite similar to the noise made by a small animal swimming across a pond. Again the sound appeal is to arouse the fish's desire to feed, for fish will eat any small animals they can catch.

These same sounds have a secondary appeal in arousing curiosity in fish, for aquatic creatures exhibit the same characteristics of most land animals in circling back to learn the cause of a noise. If that noisy lure looks like something edible, the fish is then likely to grab it.

The noise that seems to be most appealing to fish is that of the crippled minnow. An injured minnow climbs to the surface of the water where it makes a rapid "plip-plip-plip" sound as it thrashes about. This same sound can be incorporated in lures by the addition of small propellers, fore or aft or at both ends. When the lure is retrieved, the propellers spin and make that enticing "plip-plip-plip" noise.

Visibility under water is limited, and it can vary tremendously from day to day according to the turbidity. This is where the sound to "call" fish comes into play.

Suppose the under water visibility range is ten feet. That largemouth bass 20 feet off to the side of where the lure hit the water is not going to see the bait. It will, however, hear or, more correctly, through its lateral line feel the sound vibrations set up when the lure struck the water. The initial noise will alert the fish and quite likely make it suspicious. The skilled artificial lure angler will allow the lure to rest motionless for a few seconds, perhaps as much as a half minute, in order to give the fish time to overcome any fright. Then the angler goes to work with his rod and reel to put the action into the lure to produce those fish-attracting sounds.

Remember the bass still has not established visual contact with the lure. The fish is still suspicious enough to face in the direction from which the initial "plop" came, but the creature is probably wrestling with its emotions whether to swim over to investigate or turn tail for the other side of the pond. Now the fisherman puts action into his lure and the bass picks up a faint but distinct fluttering "plip-plip-plip." From past experiences the fish associates this noise with that of the crippled minnow struggling for survival at the surface of the water. Also from past experiences the fish knows a crippled minnow is an easy fellow to catch. So the fish begins to move in the direction of the sound. Soon it has made visual contact.

This is the point where game calling and fish calling take separate paths. In game calling there is no lure involved. Sound —and sound alone—brings the game within taking range of the hunter. The exceptions are with ducks, geese, and crows where decoys are set out. With the fish that has established visual contact with the lure, sounds become secondary to motion and sight. If the lure is made to perform the antics of the injured minnow, the fish will home in to make the most of what it visualizes as an easy meal.

In doing research for one of my earlier books, *Lure Fishing* (A. S. Barnes & Co., Inc., 1970), I contacted a number of lure manufacturers and questioned them about sound and its importance in attracting fish to lures. All considered sound as foremost in establishing initial contact with the fish.

As in game and bird calling, sounds applied to attract fish can be of such intensity and volume as to actually repel fish. Many fishermen who are conscious that the sounds made by their lures aid in attracting fish go too far and over do it. They manipulate their rods and reels with too much gusto. They, the fishermen, seem to feel the sound is not right unless they can hear it distinctly themselves. When they do this, they overlook that highly important property of water—its density. Being five times denser than the air above, water is an excellent conductor of sound and it will transmit sound vibrations five times the distance the same sound would carry in the air. So what does this mean? The fisherman who viciously pops his rod to get what he regards as a pleasing "chug" to his ears is actually producing a hard, sudden bomb-like noise to nearby fish. The result is the fish bolt and fin out of the immediate area.

From time to time various mechanical so-called "fish calls" have been put on the market. All make the same basic sound—

a "tick-tick-tick." By means of a dial the operator can speed up the "tick-tick-tick" until it becomes a buzz. There is no question about fish being able to hear or feel these noises. Whether these devices actually call fish or not is a moot question. Personally I feel the noise serves to attract fish more on the basis of mesmerism than anything else. I do not feel it triggers them to feed. If the fish happen to be hungry at the time bait is dangled around the "fish-caller," they will start to feed.

I have experimented with these gadgets on a number of occasions. I have yet to be successful in having the sound, whether it is a slow "tick-tick-tick" or a bee "buzz," attract fish of any appreciable size. The devices have been successful in pulling in schools of small baitfish many times. But schools of big fish, no. At least not for me.

Of course, in fairness to the fellows who strive to perfect these gadgets, I must confess that I may be prejudiced. Back in the early 1960s outdoors writers around the country were bombarded with letters offering for "field testing" an electronic "fish-caller." The device operated off a penlight cell and produced sounds ranging from the "tick-tick-tick" to a rattlesnake "buzz." The item was an import, and someone from the land of the Japanese did an excellent job in lining up a flock of jobbers in the good old U.S.A. I received no less than 37 letters offering free "fish-callers" for "field testing" purposes. I answered one of the letters and fiddled with the device on a half dozen fishing trips. The results on each trip were blah. It would be an injustice to honest fishermen to term the results unimpressive. Nevertheless, some months later in some printed advertising I saw on the same device I noted the line: "used by scores of famous outdoors writers, names on request." I was curious, and so on plain stationery I requested a list of the "famous outdoors writers." In due time I received the list and there was my name on it. "Famous" is an ethereal word. It is like the color gray—any shade between white and black. The advertising merely mentioned "used by." It did not state that the writers endorsed the product. However, the copy writer made hay out of a trait so many folks have in the tendency to read an advertisement not as it is written but as they would like it to sound. If I sound a little prejudiced, I believe I have legitimate cause.

Now let's get on to some of the proven sounds that do produce fish. These sounds can be produced by surface lures, certain sub-surface lures, and specially designed fishing floats.

Lures with concave and saucer-like faces produce the "chugs" and "plops," depending upon the force the angler applies in popping his rod. The sounds are very similar to those made when large fish feed on the surface. The idea here appears to be that if the fish hear other fish-eating sounds they ought to hurry over to join in on the feast.

Plugs with inverted lips, like the popular Arbogast Jitterbug, "surgle" as they are retrieved. This is supposed to represent the noise of a small animal swimming. It is also a sound not unlike that made by a large frog swimming on the surface. Lures with propellers make the rapid "plip-plip-plip" associated with the erratic and frantic struggling of the crippled minnow.

Sinking plugs that wiggle violently when retrieved employ sound to attract fish. The wiggle, which in some lures is so fast that it could be called vibration, sets up sound waves that are felt through a fish's lateral line. Good examples of this type of lure are the Heddon Sonic and the Heddon SuperSonic.

That specialized float that produces fish-attracting sounds is called the "popping cork." It is widely used throughout the Gulf Coast States in fishing the shallow salt-water bays. Originally the float was made out of cork, hence the name "popping cork." To-day these same floats are made almost exclusively from plastic or Styrofoam, although the old name still prevails. The float has a concave top. At rest the float rides upright in the water. When the rod tip is popped sharply the float will tip over with the con-cave top digging into the surface. The resulting sound is either a "chug" or a "plop," depending upon the force applied to the rod. The sound is like that of the fishing plug mentioned earlier in this chapter, only in the case of the float the noise is deeper and louder. This is necessary if it is to be heard above the usual noises so prevalent in salt-water fishing. The float is not used in fresh-water fishing for the resulting noises are generally too harsh. It takes a long, whippy rod to put the right action in this float, and over the years a special rod has been developed for fishing the "popping cork." It is no surprise that the rod is re-ferred to as a "popping rod."

26.

Wildlife Photography

THE WIDESPREAD PUBLICITY WITH THE RESULTING ATTENTION GIVEN to our shrinking wilderness, extinct animal and bird species, and the growing list of endangered wildlife species has kindled great interest in the outdoors. The problems have aroused the curiosity of many folks who have had their interest whetted to the extent that they want to see for themselves. So they go to the fields and forests seeking animals and birds not with guns but simply to observe. Some do more than just observe. They seek to record the panorama on film.

The problem of recording wild animals and birds on film has always been one of getting the creatures close. The telephoto lens gives the photographer a lot of reach into the distance, but these lenses have their drawbacks. For one thing the photo of a snarling fox snapped through a telephoto lens at a distance of 100 yards just does not have the same exciting appeal of a photo of the same animal taken from a distance of 25 feet. If a fellow is interested simply in building up a run-of-the-mill photo collection of wild creatures, the telephoto lens will give him all he wants. But if he wants that collection to have a special snap, photos that clearly show an animal's raised hackles, the glow in its eyes, or its teeth in bold relief, he must get the animal in close —certainly inside of 50 feet. This is where the telephoto lens can really pull your game up close. The resulting photo, of course, may not include the entire animal, but it will give the photographer a detailed close-up of whatever portion of the critter he desires to photograph.

One can depend upon luck or skill to get the creatures inside of those 50 feet. If you put your faith in luck, expect some

135

mighty long waits between pictures. You can save a lot of time and get better pictures as well if you put your faith in skillful use of the game, bird, or fowl call. These calls, when properly used, can pull the creatures in close enough for photography with the normal lens.

When one starts talking about cameras, and especially cameras equipped with telephoto lenses, a lot of folks get an uneasy feeling in their stomachs. They can just see the cash register running up figures in the direction of the national debt. The professional outdoors photographer will own equipment representing an investment of thousands of dollars. This is necessary since he must turn out professional-quality photos if he expects to sell them.

The outdoorsman who seeks to build up a wildlife photo collection simply as a hobby can get by adequately with an investment of approximately $300 for camera equipment. If he decides to set up his own temporary darkroom in his bathroom at home, he can figure on spending another hundred bucks. And for still another hundred he can set up a semi-permanent darkroom at home. Let's disregard the home darkroom project and run through the $300 for camera equipment and see what a fellow can purchase.

On the camera itself—and this means camera body with the normal lens—he can go one of three routes. He can go twin lens reflex in the 2¼ by 2¼ format, 35 millimeter with split image rangefinder, or 35 mm single lens reflex (also called through lens). Each of the three mounts will take an assortment of telephoto lens. The least expensive system is the twin lens reflex, next is the 35 mm camera with the split image rangefinder, and the SLR is the most expensive of the lot. This holds for what are known as "popular brand" cameras. You can get some "Rolls Royce" equipment in any of the three lines, but you will also pay some mighty high prices.

All three of the systems mentioned will produce quality photos if the user masters the necessary skills and techniques. However, when it comes to outdoors photographic work, the SLR camera holds marked advantages over the other two systems.

When it comes to photographing wild animals and birds, especially if they are close, operation speed is of the utmost importance. When the game hears the shutter snap, it is not going to tarry around to ask questions. It is going to high-tail for parts on the other side of the hill. This right here rules out the twin lens reflex camera. Too much time is necessary to advance the film for additional photos. Furthermore, to advance film in this type camera it is necessary to make considerable hand movement in turning the film crank. This motion can be enough to spook the game if it misses hearing the shutter snap. An additional drawback with this camera is that it is slow to focus, and critical focus is an absolute must if one is to obtain sharp pictures.

The 35 mm camera with split image rangefinder can be operated rapidly. Yet it, too, has a serious drawback when it comes to wildlife photography. The problem here will be in focusing on the object. In poor light and particularly in wooded areas it is often difficult to focus with the split image rangefinder. You can advance film and shoot rapidly, but you are likely to end up with a lot of out-of-focus pictures.

The preference of most outdoors photographers is the SLR system. You observe the game you plan to photograph right through the lens thanks to a system of mirrors within the camera body. The system gives you the advantage of composing your picture, for you see in the viewfinder exactly what will appear in the finished photo. Focusing is simply a matter of getting a sharp image in the viewfinder, and this by far beats trying to line up split images in such a manner that they become one. If the image you see in the SLR viewfinder is blurred, then it is out of focus. Simply turn the focusing system until the image pops up clear and sharp. It is just that simple.

A good "brand name" SLR camera with the normal 50 mm or 55mm lens can be purchased new in a price range of $125 to $200. A good used camera of the same brand will sell for 30 to 40 percent less. How high the price goes on any camera will depend upon how many extra refinements or gadgets you desire on the basic camera body. The normal lens will be suitable for photographing fox-size or larger game up to about 100 feet distance. Beyond that a telephoto lens will be necessary.

A good "brand name" 200 mm to 400 mm telephoto lens can be purchased in a $75 to $125 price range. These lenses will serve the hobbyist, although most professional photographers won't settle for anything less than a $300 lens. It is your money so spend it as you see fit. Just keep in mind that high price equipment is not the real answer to quality photographs. It is the skill of the bug who works the camera that really gets the results. For telephoto work involving large-size animals, a 200 mm lens will do the job quite well. Where birdlife is concerned, the 200 mm lens is the smallest acceptable size. The 300 mm and 400 mm lens are far better choices. Telephoto lenses larger than 400 mm are often difficult for the amateur photographer to handle. The tiniest motion or vibration within the camera is certain to show up on the film in the form of blurring when ultra-long barreled lenses are employed. These lenses require a steady platform.

There is one lens of tremendous value to the outdoorsman who can afford only a single camera. The lens I refer to is the zoom, which is available for both still and movie cameras. The zoom gives the single camera owner the versatility of several formats within a single lens system. The range of most zoom lenses for SLR cameras is 85 mm to 210 mm with settings in between at 105 mm, 135 mm, and 180 mm. This in effect gives the photographer five lenses in one. Consider the options he has in taking pictures. For example, suppose at 85 mm he gets a picture of the deer in its natural surroundings. Another shot at 105 mm brings the deer larger with less surrounding countryside. At the far end of the range—210 mm—the photographer gets an extreme close-up of the deer only. The surrounding countryside is cut out.

Without a zoom lens, the photographer in order to get the same set of pictures would have to own five separate lenses. He would have to change lenses for each picture, and since lens changing is more than just a flick of the wrists, the odds are poor for the deer to remain around long enough for the fellow to go through five lens changes.

The zoom lens advantage is flexibility and economy. It also has its disadvantages. It will not produce photos as sharp as the fixed focal length lenses. This, however, will not be noticed unless you intend to make extremely big enlargements. The zoom will suffice if you blow up your 35 mm negatives to 8 by 10 size. When you start going 11 by 14 and larger, distortions will show up in the finished photo. A zoom lens that will give satisfactory results as long as you stay in the the 8 by 10 photo size can be had in a price range of $100 to $150. If you purchased a separate lens for each of the settings on the zoom lens, you would own five lenses. The cost for these five lenses would be in the vicinity of $300.

Whether you use the fixed focal length telephoto lens or the zoom, by all means purchase a system that is marked as "automatic." When focusing through the automatic lens, the lens is wide open allowing you to view the subject in the most light available. When you shoot the picture and just a split fraction of a second before the shutter is tripped, the automatic device in the lens stops the aperture down to the proper opening for the existing light condition, which is determined by use of a light meter. With the lens marked as "pre-set" you have to focus with the aperture wide open and then manually stop down the aperture before snapping the picture. Meanwhile in the time elapsed doing all this, the deer has probably already gone to the other side of the hill. Most automatic lenses cost approximately 50 percent more than their pre-set counterparts. It is poor economy to go with anything less than automatic. The pre-set lens has its place in photography but that place is not in either outdoors or sports photography.

By all means use film that will accomplish your mission. When buying film consider the finished product you desire, and don't let price alone dictate your ultimate purchase. All film comes with a basic ASA (American Standards Association) index. This keys the film as to whether it is fast or slow. The professional photographer who operates his own darkroom can greatly increase film ratings to make it faster for use in poor light situations. He does the altering with the types of chemical developers he uses. This is what is known as "pushing" film. For example, you can push Tri-X film, which is normally rated at ASA 400, to an ASA equivalent to 2400 by the kind of developer used. This push in film speed will allow you to take photos under extremely poor light conditions. Be prepared, however, to accept losses in quality in your photographs. These losses, in unusually big enlargements, will be most critical in definition and grain.

It is far better to buy special film for that special purpose than it is to attempt to make normal film perform a special purpose through chemical "pushing." The extra price for special film more than compensates for quality losses that may occur through the use of standard film that is "pushed."

Lighting presents all sorts of weird problems for the outdoors photographer. If he takes a light meter reading for each individual picture he snaps, he will spend half his time afield adjusting aperture openings and shutter speeds. This will be especially true if his photography is done in the woods where light conditions can vary from minute to minute. Light conditions often depend upon which way a tree leans in the wind.

You can take a meter reading for each individual picture. Just be prepared to miss a lot of shots when the animal vanishes in the time it took you to take a meter reading and then adjust the settings on the camera. You may want to adopt the system I use.

I take a meter reading when I get on location and set my camera accordingly. Then when the subject comes into view and into the setting where I want to snap the picture, I try to get off three pictures. The first will be at the setting determined by the light meter, the second at an aperture stop above this reading, and the third at a stop below the light meter reading. This is known as "bracketing." It is a case of playing the odds that one of the three negatives will be correctly exposed. Since I do my own darkroom work, I can make each of the three negatives work for me simply by compensating in exposure times in the enlarger. "Bracketing" is the best insurance a photographer has in that it guarantees he will get at least one usable picture.

Under normal conditions the cheapest item in photography is film. When it comes to outdoor photography, consider film— even color film—as being even less expensive. In studio photography as well as in the garden variety of family picture taking, you can always do it again if the picture does not come out. The only thing lost is a little time. That deer in the brush, the fox tip-toeing on the rocks across the stream, and the mallard about to land in the decoys are not going to come back tomorrow to give you a second chance if your film today did not turn out just right.

Every time you focus your camera on a wild animal or bird, view it as an incident never to occur again. Then shoot and use up film as if the stuff was going out of style. I have in my collection of outdoors photos some that I have never been able to come near duplicating. Look at it this way. You can get a picture of the baby smiling by tickling the child. Or if you want the baby to cry, you pinch its bottom. Neither animals nor birds will permit you to take similar liberties for those special expression photos.

In addition to the camera with the normal and telephoto lenses, the only other major item necessary is a good tripod. You can do without the tripod when using the normal 50 mm or 55 mm lenses. You can use the telephoto lens and get by without using the tripod if the light is real good, for then you can use a fast 1/500 or 1/1000 shutter speed. However, when you start shooting the long lens at shutter speeds of 1/200 or slower, you are almost certain to get blurred photos because of camera movement or vibration.

The tripod gives the photographer an excellent platform that can be the initial step toward making exceptionally sharp photos. As an illustration, suppose the fellow is working a varmint call and notes a coyote approaching in his direction. He can plot the animal's likely approach and pretty well figure where it will come out of the brush. All he needs to do is aim the camera at that spot, draw critical focus, and wait for the animal to reveal itself.

Another advantage of the tripod is that it takes a lot of weight off the user. Instead of hanging around his neck, swinging in the way, or bumping against the tree trunk, the camera is out of the way on the tripod. The outdoorsman is thusly freed of a burden that could hamper his use of the game call.

Purchase a tripod that has a head that permits both vertical and horizontal panning. Make sure you get one with sturdy legs, for a camera with a telephoto lens is a pretty weighty instrument. You don't want a tripod that will fall over under the weight. Repairing dropped cameras and lenses can be very costly.

Index

Alligators, 74–75
American Indians, 13, 67
Arbogast Jitterbug, 134
Assembly call for
  chukars, 48
  pheasants, 47
  quail, 49–50
  turkeys, 36–37
Attraction calls, 15, 16, 19, 26, 39, 84,
  100, 119, 120, 130

Bears, 56, 61
Blinds, 55, 105–109
  approach to, 106
  concealment in, 108
  silhouettes, 105
Bluejays, 34, 103
Bobcats, 42, 72, 75, 89, 91, 104

Camouflage clothes, 31, 54, 99, 102,
  105
Canada, 45
Car honking game, 123
Central America, 56
Chukars, 48–49, 91
  assembly call for, 48
  call sequence for, 48
  characteristics of, 48
  time to call for, 49
Cleaning calls, 128–129
Coin clicking call, 118
Coons (raccoons), 28, 42, 61, 69, 71
Copano Bay, Texas, 86
Corpus Christi, Texas, 86
Cougars, 42, 56, 61
Coy-dog, 46
Coyotes, 17, 39, 42, 44, 46, 67, 72, 89,
  95, 120
Cricket chirp range, 66
Cripple-stopper shot, 29
Crows, 42, 52–55, 71, 89, 91, 95, 103,
  115, 122
  decoys for, 53, 54

distress call for, 53, 95
electronic calls for, 54, 115
fight call for, 53, 95
Curiosity of wildlife, 39, 59, 62–63, 84,
  90, 119

Deer, 39, 59–60, 61, 69, 72–73, 85, 91,
  100, 119, 120, 122
  curiosity of, 39, 59, 119
  doe calls, 60
  horn-rattling for, 59, 100
  sounds made by, 59, 72–73
Distinguishing colors by wildlife, 99,
  105, 108
Doves, 16, 91
Ducks, 13, 18–23, 26, 35, 54, 62, 74,
  77–78, 85, 86, 91, 96, 99, 111–12,
  114, 129
  alarm call by, 23
  attraction call for, 19
  comeback call for, 21
  decoys for, 18, 20, 86, 89
  feeding chuckle for, 19, 20, 22
  hail call for, 20
  mallard drake call, 21, 77
  mallard hen call, 21, 62, 77
  reach of calls for, 19, 22
  species of, 21
  talk back call for, 21
  when to call, 19

Electronic calls, 38, 54, 68, 111, 114–
  16, 117
  crows, 54
  turkeys, 38
  varmints, 46
Elk, 58, 66, 73, 89, 91, 100
  bugling for, 58, 66, 89
  challenge call for, 58
  sounds made by, 73

Feeding periods, 94–95
Fishing, 83, 116, 124, 130–34

143